The Tempest
Annotation-Friendly Edition

William Shakespeare

This book is also available in large-print, extra large print and dyslexia-friendly editions

firestonebooks.com

The Tempest
Annotation-Friendly Edition
William Shakespeare

2019 Edition

Published by Firestone Books

ISBN-13: 9781796820805

firestonebooks.com

You can also find out more by following Firestone Books on Facebook and Twitter

CONTENTS

A Quick Guide to Successful Annotating

- Write down any thoughts you have as you go along
- Highlight key points, either with a highlighter or by underlining
- Note any literary techniques in the margins. (The *Glossary of Literary Terms* at the back of the book should help)
- Define any words you don't understand – it will help you later
- Look for patterns, such as repeating words and phrases
- Pick out key points that show a character's development
- Summarise your thoughts on the blank pages at the end of each act
- Once you've finished reading the play, go back and add to your notes. In particular look at foreshadowing, echoing and motifs

William Shakespeare – A Brief Biography

William Shakespeare was born in Stratford-upon-Avon, the son of John Shakespeare, a successful glove-maker, and Mary Arden, the daughter of a prosperous farmer. His date of birth is unknown but he was baptised, most likely within a few days of his birth, on 26th April 1564.

It is likely that Shakespeare attended the King's New School in Stratford-upon-Avon where he would have received a classical education. He did not attend university, and at the age of eighteen he married Anne Hathaway who was eight years his senior. Six months later, in May 1583, Anne gave birth to a daughter, Susanna. In 1585 Anne also gave birth to twins, Hamnet and Judith.

Between 1585 and 1592 almost nothing is known of Shakespeare's life, the so called "lost years". Many apocryphal tales about this period have been reported including that he fled his hometown for London to escape prosecution for deer poaching, that he started his theatrical career minding the horses of wealthy theatregoers, and that he may have been briefly employed as a schoolmaster in Lancashire.

By 1592 Shakespeare was an established playwright, with several of his plays having been staged in London. It is also the year that fellow playwright, Robert Greene, published his infamous *Groats-Worth of Wit* in which he attacked Shakespeare for trying to match the writing of university educated writers such as Christopher Marlowe and Thomas Nashe.

Shakespeare's plays were only performed by the Lord Chamberlain's Men, a company of actors, in which Shakespeare had a share.

In 1596, Shakespeare's only son, Hamnet, died, and

while in later years Shakespeare's daughters would marry and have four children between them, none of Shakespeare's grandchildren would have children of their own, and so in 1670 with the death of his granddaughter, Elizabeth, his direct line was ended.

In 1599 some members of the Lord Chamberlain's Men built their own theatre on the south bank of the river Thames and named it the Globe. As a shareholder in this theatre, holding up to 3000 spectators, Shakespeare became a wealthy man.

Prior to 1599 Shakespeare had only written two tragedies: *Titus Andronicus* and *Romeo and Juliet*, with his focus being more on comedies, history plays and poems. After 1599 he almost stopped writing history plays and instead switched to writing tragedies, writing many of his finest plays including: *Hamlet, Othello, King Lear* and *Macbeth*.

In 1603 the new king, James I, awarded the Lord Chamberlain's Men a royal patent and the company changed its name to the King's Men.

As well as writing plays, Shakespeare also wrote two long poems and a collection of sonnets. The sonnets describe two love affairs, but who these lovers were – or even if they were real or imagined – remains a mystery.

As Shakespeare was also an actor, it meant that rather than working on his plays in isolation he would have worked closely with other actors. Many of the plots for the plays came from history books, or earlier Italian tales, so it is difficult, if not impossible, to work out what contributions were Shakespeare's. Even when he'd finished a particular play, it was still likely to be re-worked by actors and others – something that is done to this day and keeps his work as fresh and interesting as its ever been.

Though Shakespeare worked as a writer and actor

in London for most of his adult life, his did spend much of his time in Stratford-upon-Avon where, in 1597, he bought New Place as his family home. It's known that Shakespeare was still working as an actor in London in 1608, and that he also retired to Stratford 'some years before his death'.

Shakespeare died on the 23rd of April 1616, around the time of his 52nd birthday. It was said by John Ward, the vicar of Stratford, writing in the mid-1600s that 'Shakespeare, Drayton and Ben Johnson had a merry meeting and, it seems, drank too hard, for Shakespeare died of a fever there contracted.'

Shakespeare was buried at the Holy Trinity Church, the place of his baptism over half a century earlier. The epitaph on his gravestone has a curse against disturbing his resting place:

Good friend, for Jesus' sake forbear,
To dig the dust enclosed here.
Blessed be the man that spares these stones,
And cursed be he that moves my bones.

Fellow dramatist, Ben Johnson, famously and presciently referred to Shakespeare as being 'not of an age, but for all time.' Since his death Shakespeare's reputation has grown, leading him to now be widely regarded as the greatest writer in the English language and the world's greatest dramatist.

Introduction

The Tempest is almost certainly the last play written solely by Shakespeare, and is seen as something of a swansong.

Most likely written in either 1610 or 1611, the year of its first known performance, *The Tempest* seems to have been based on a number of sources including the Italian Commedia dell'arte, Jakob Ayrer's *Comedia von der Schöne Sidea* (*Comedy of the Beautiful Sidea*), Michel de Montaigne's essay *Of the Canibales* and numerous accounts of shipwrecks such as William Strachey's *A True Report of the Wracke and Redemption of Sir Thomas Gates, Knight* and Sylvester Jourdain's *A Discovery of the Barmudas*.

Spoiler alert – if you do not know what happens in *The Tempest*, you may wish to stop reading the introduction now and return to it after reading the play.

The Tempest has numerous themes running throughout, with a variety of allusions to the theatre, and many critics and scholars from at least the time of critic Thomas Campbell in 1838 have seen these theatrical references, not least Prospero's renunciation of magic towards the end of the play, as Shakespeare signalling his farewell to the stage.

Magic is a theme that is also runs through the play. While this may not seem particularly interesting or shocking to modern audiences, in Shakespeare's time when the play was written, magic was seen as a dangerous and ungodly topic. To many of the time such supernatural powers could only spring from the devil, and for Shakespeare to have presented a good character with such powers may have appeared to some as wrong and anti-Christian. To offset this, Sycorax is presented as a devil-worshipping magician, in contrast to Prospero who only uses his magic for good, and ultimately renounces it.

Set on a distant island, perhaps in the Caribbean, colonisation is also a subject that *The Tempest* touches on. *The Tempest* was written at a time when much of the New World was being colonised by European settlers, and many myths were brought back, with tales of cannibals and the like. Indeed, the deformed slave, Caliban, one of the most distinctive characters in any of Shakespeare's plays, may have a name derived from cannibal (of which it is almost an anagram) and also resembles "Cariban" the term then used for a Caribbean native.

The Tempest is unusual by Shakespeare's standards, not only due to its short length, but also due to its being set at one place, and the action happening in real time, that is to say that rather than taking place over weeks or months it takes place in just a few hours.

The play is also one that not only entertains, but also begs and number of questions: Is Ariel male or does "he" have a more ambiguous gender? Is it right to classify *The Tempest* as a comedy? Was *The Tempest* really Shakespeare's way of saying goodbye to the theatre? Is it a problem that the play only has one female character? It is Prospero who portrays Caliban's mother, Sycorax, in a negative light, but can we take his word for it given he has never met her? Does the play's title refer to more than the initial storm – is there metaphorical significance?

As well as having been adapted for stage and screen many times, *The Tempest,* with its dramatic and exotic scenery has inspired painters and writers, it has been turned into ballets and operas, poems and pop songs. This brilliant play has inspired and entertained people for centuries and doubtless will continue to do so for centuries to come.

THE
TEMPEST

Dramatis Personae

ALONSO, King of Naples

SEBASTIAN, his brother

PROSPERO, the right Duke of Milan

ANTONIO, his Brother, the usurping Duke of Milan

FERDINAND, Son to the King of Naples

GONZALO, an honest old Counsellor

ADRIAN, Lord

FRANCISCO, Lord

CALIBAN, a savage and deformed Slave

TRINCULO, a Jester

STEPHANO, a drunken Butler

Master of a Ship, Boatswain, Mariners

MIRANDA, Daughter to Prospero

IRIS, presented by Spirits

CERES, presented by Spirits

JUNO, presented by Spirits

Nymphs, presented by Spirits

Reapers, presented by Spirits

Other Spirits attending on Prospero

ACT I

SCENE I – On a ship at sea. A tempestuous noise of thunder and lightning heard.

[*Enter a Master and a Boatswain*]
Master: Boatswain!
Boatswain: Here, master: what cheer?
Master: Good, speak to the mariners: fall to't, yarely, or we run ourselves aground: bestir, bestir.
[*Exit*]
[*Enter Mariners*]
Boatswain: Heigh, my hearts! cheerly, cheerly, my hearts! yare, yare! Take in the topsail. Tend to the master's whistle. Blow, till thou burst thy wind, if room enough!
[*Enter ALONSO, SEBASTIAN, ANTONIO, FERDINAND, GONZALO, and others*]
ALONSO: Good boatswain, have care. Where's
10 the master? Play the men.
Boatswain: I pray now, keep below.
ANTONIO: Where is the master, boatswain?
Boatswain: Do you not hear him? You mar our

labour: keep your cabins: you do assist the
storm.

GONZALO: Nay, good, be patient.

Boatswain: When the sea is. Hence! What
cares these roarers for the name of king? To
cabin: silence! trouble us not.

GONZALO: Good, yet remember whom thou
hast aboard.

Boatswain: None that I more love than myself.
You are a counsellor; if you can command these
elements to silence, and work the peace of the
present, we will not hand a rope more; use your
authority: if you cannot, give thanks you have
lived so long, and make yourself ready in your
cabin for the mischance of the hour, if it so hap.
Cheerly, good hearts! Out of our way, I say.
[*Exit*]

GONZALO: I have great comfort from this fellow:
methinks he hath no drowning mark upon him;
his complexion is perfect gallows. Stand fast,
good Fate, to his hanging: make the rope of his
destiny our cable, for our own doth little
advantage. If he be not born to be hanged, our
case is miserable.

[Exeunt]

[Re-enter Boatswain]

Boatswain: Down with the topmast! yare! lower, lower! Bring her to try with main-course.

[A cry within]

A plague upon this howling! they are louder than the weather or our office.

[Re-enter SEBASTIAN, ANTONIO, and GONZALO]

Yet again! what do you here? Shall we give o'er and drown? Have you a mind to sink?

SEBASTIAN: A pox o' your throat, you bawling, blasphemous, incharitable dog!

Boatswain: Work you then.

ANTONIO: Hang, cur! hang, you whoreson, insolent noisemaker!

We are less afraid to be drowned than thou art.

GONZALO: I'll warrant him for drowning; though the ship were no stronger than a nutshell and as leaky as an unstanched wench.

Boatswain: Lay her a-hold, a-hold! set her two courses off to sea again; lay her off.

[Enter Mariners wet]

Mariners: All lost! to prayers, to prayers! all lost!

Boatswain: What, must our mouths be cold?

GONZALO: The king and prince at prayers! let's assist them,

For our case is as theirs.

SEBASTIAN: I'm out of patience.

ANTONIO: We are merely cheated of our lives by drunkards:

This wide-chapp'd rascal-would thou mightst lie drowning

The washing of ten tides!

GONZALO: He'll be hang'd yet,

Though every drop of water swear against it

And gape at widest to glut him.

[*A confused noise within: 'Mercy on us!'- 'We split, we split!'-'Farewell, my wife and children!'-'Farewell, brother!'-'We split, we split, we split!'*]

ANTONIO: Let's all sink with the king.

SEBASTIAN: Let's take leave of him.

[*Exeunt ANTONIO and SEBASTIAN*]

GONZALO: Now would I give a thousand furlongs of sea for an acre of barren ground, long heath, brown furze, any thing. The wills above be done! but I would fain die a dry death.

[*Exeunt*]

SCENE II – The island. Before Prospero's cell.

[Enter PROSPERO and MIRANDA]

MIRANDA: If by your art, my dearest father, you have
Put the wild waters in this roar, allay them.
The sky, it seems, would pour down stinking pitch,
But that the sea, mounting to the welkin's cheek,
Dashes the fire out. O, I have suffered
With those that I saw suffer: a brave vessel,
Who had, no doubt, some noble creature in her,
Dash'd all to pieces. O, the cry did knock
Against my very heart. Poor souls, they perish'd.
Had I been any god of power, I would
Have sunk the sea within the earth or ere
It should the good ship so have swallow'd and
The fraughting souls within her.

PROSPERO: Be collected:
No more amazement: tell your piteous heart
There's no harm done.

MIRANDA: O, woe the day!

PROSPERO: No harm.
I have done nothing but in care of thee,

Of thee, my dear one, thee, my daughter, who

Art ignorant of what thou art, nought knowing

Of whence I am, nor that I am more better

Than Prospero, master of a full poor cell,

And thy no greater father.

MIRANDA: More to know

Did never meddle with my thoughts.

PROSPERO: 'Tis time

I should inform thee farther. Lend thy hand,

And pluck my magic garment from me. So:

[*Lays down his mantle*]

Lie there, my art. Wipe thou thine eyes; have

comfort.

The direful spectacle of the wreck, which touch'd

The very virtue of compassion in thee,

I have with such provision in mine art

So safely ordered that there is no soul-

No, not so much perdition as an hair

Betid to any creature in the vessel

Which thou heard'st cry, which thou saw'st sink.

Sit down;

For thou must now know farther.

MIRANDA: You have often

Begun to tell me what I am, but stopp'd

And left me to a bootless inquisition,

Concluding 'Stay: not yet.'

PROSPERO: The hour's now come;

The very minute bids thee ope thine ear;

Obey and be attentive. Canst thou remember

A time before we came unto this cell?

I do not think thou canst, for then thou wast not

Out three years old.

MIRANDA: Certainly, sir, I can.

PROSPERO: By what? by any other house or

person?

Of any thing the image tell me that

Hath kept with thy remembrance.

MIRANDA: 'Tis far off

And rather like a dream than an assurance

That my remembrance warrants. Had I not

Four or five women once that tended me?

PROSPERO: Thou hadst, and more, Miranda.

But how is it

That this lives in thy mind? What seest thou else

In the dark backward and abysm of time?

If thou remember'st aught ere thou camest here,

How thou camest here thou mayst.

MIRANDA: But that I do not.

PROSPERO: Twelve year since, Miranda,
twelve year since,
Thy father was the Duke of Milan and
A prince of power.

MIRANDA: Sir, are not you my father?

PROSPERO: Thy mother was a piece of virtue,
and
She said thou wast my daughter; and thy father
Was Duke of Milan; and thou his only heir
And princess no worse issued.

MIRANDA: O the heavens!
What foul play had we, that we came from
thence?
Or blessed was't we did?

PROSPERO: Both, both, my girl:
By foul play, as thou say'st, were we heaved
thence,
But blessedly holp hither.

MIRANDA: O, my heart bleeds
To think o' the teen that I have turn'd you to,
Which is from my remembrance! Please you,
farther.

PROSPERO: My brother and thy uncle, call'd
Antonio-

I pray thee, mark me-that a brother should

Be so perfidious!-he whom next thyself

Of all the world I loved and to him put

The manage of my state; as at that time

Through all the signories it was the first

And Prospero the prime duke, being so reputed

In dignity, and for the liberal arts

Without a parallel; those being all my study,

The government I cast upon my brother

And to my state grew stranger, being transported

And rapt in secret studies. Thy false uncle-

Dost thou attend me?

MIRANDA: Sir, most heedfully.

PROSPERO: Being once perfected how to grant

suits,

How to deny them, who to advance and who

To trash for over-topping, new created

The creatures that were mine, I say, or changed

'em,

Or else new form'd 'em; having both the key

Of officer and office, set all hearts i' the state

To what tune pleased his ear; that now he was

The ivy which had hid my princely trunk,

And suck'd my verdure out on't. Thou attend'st

not.

MIRANDA: O, good sir, I do.

PROSPERO: I pray thee, mark me.

I, thus neglecting worldly ends, all dedicated

To closeness and the bettering of my mind

With that which, but by being so retired,

O'er-prized all popular rate, in my false brother

Awaked an evil nature; and my trust,

Like a good parent, did beget of him

A falsehood in its contrary as great

As my trust was; which had indeed no limit,

A confidence sans bound. He being thus lorded,

Not only with what my revenue yielded,

But what my power might else exact, like one

Who having into truth, by telling of it,

Made such a sinner of his memory,

To credit his own lie, he did believe

He was indeed the duke; out o' the substitution

And executing the outward face of royalty,

With all prerogative: hence his ambition growing-

Dost thou hear?

MIRANDA: Your tale, sir, would cure deafness.

PROSPERO: To have no screen between this

part he play'd

And him he play'd it for, he needs will be

Absolute Milan. Me, poor man, my library

Was dukedom large enough: of temporal

royalties

He thinks me now incapable; confederates-

So dry he was for sway-wi' the King of Naples

To give him annual tribute, do him homage,

Subject his coronet to his crown and bend

The dukedom yet unbow'd-alas, poor Milan!

To most ignoble stooping.

MIRANDA: O the heavens!

PROSPERO: Mark his condition and the event;

then tell me

If this might be a brother.

MIRANDA: I should sin

To think but nobly of my grandmother:

Good wombs have borne bad sons.

PROSPERO: Now the condition.

The King of Naples, being an enemy

To me inveterate, hearkens my brother's suit;

Which was, that he, in lieu o' the premises

Of homage and I know not how much tribute,

Should presently extirpate me and mine

Out of the dukedom and confer fair Milan

With all the honours on my brother: whereon,

A treacherous army levied, one midnight

Fated to the purpose did Antonio open

The gates of Milan, and, i' the dead of darkness,

The ministers for the purpose hurried thence

Me and thy crying self.

MIRANDA: Alack, for pity!

I, not remembering how I cried out then,

Will cry it o'er again: it is a hint

That wrings mine eyes to't.

PROSPERO: Hear a little further

And then I'll bring thee to the present business

Which now's upon's; without the which this story

Were most impertinent.

MIRANDA: Wherefore did they not

That hour destroy us?

PROSPERO: Well demanded, wench:

My tale provokes that question. Dear, they durst

not,

So dear the love my people bore me, nor set

A mark so bloody on the business, but

With colours fairer painted their foul ends.

In few, they hurried us aboard a bark,

Bore us some leagues to sea; where they

prepared

A rotten carcass of a boat, not rigg'd,

Nor tackle, sail, nor mast; the very rats

Instinctively had quit it: there they hoist us,

To cry to the sea that roar'd to us, to sigh

To the winds whose pity, sighing back again,

Did us but loving wrong.

MIRANDA: Alack, what trouble

Was I then to you!

PROSPERO: O, a cherubim

Thou wast that did preserve me. Thou didst smile.

Infused with a fortitude from heaven,

When I have deck'd the sea with drops full salt,

Under my burden groan'd; which raised in me

An undergoing stomach, to bear up

Against what should ensue.

MIRANDA: How came we ashore?

PROSPERO: By Providence divine.

Some food we had and some fresh water that

A noble Neapolitan, Gonzalo,

Out of his charity, being then appointed

Master of this design, did give us, with

Rich garments, linens, stuffs and necessaries,

Which since have steaded much; so, of his gentleness,

Knowing I loved my books, he furnish'd me

From mine own library with volumes that

I prize above my dukedom.

MIRANDA: Would I might

But ever see that man!

PROSPERO: Now I arise:

[*Resumes his mantle*]

Sit still, and hear the last of our sea-sorrow.

Here in this island we arrived; and here

Have I, thy schoolmaster, made thee more profit

Than other princesses can that have more time

For vainer hours and tutors not so careful.

MIRANDA: Heavens thank you for't! And now, I pray you, sir,

For still 'tis beating in my mind, your reason

For raising this sea-storm?

PROSPERO: Know thus far forth.

By accident most strange, bountiful Fortune,

Now my dear lady, hath mine enemies

Brought to this shore; and by my prescience

I find my zenith doth depend upon

A most auspicious star, whose influence

If now I court not but omit, my fortunes
Will ever after droop. Here cease more
questions:
Thou art inclined to sleep; 'tis a good dulness,
And give it way: I know thou canst not choose.
[*MIRANDA sleeps*]
Come away, servant, come. I am ready now.
Approach, my Ariel, come.
[*Enter ARIEL*]
ARIEL: All hail, great master! grave sir, hail! I
come
To answer thy best pleasure; be't to fly,
To swim, to dive into the fire, to ride
On the curl'd clouds, to thy strong bidding task
Ariel and all his quality.
PROSPERO: Hast thou, spirit,
Perform'd to point the tempest that I bade thee?
ARIEL: To every article.
I boarded the king's ship; now on the beak,
Now in the waist, the deck, in every cabin,
I flamed amazement: sometime I'ld divide,
And burn in many places; on the topmast,
The yards and bowsprit, would I flame distinctly,
Then meet and join. Jove's lightnings, the

precursors

O' the dreadful thunder-claps, more momentary

And sight-outrunning were not; the fire and

cracks

Of sulphurous roaring the most mighty Neptune

Seem to besiege and make his bold waves

tremble,

Yea, his dread trident shake.

PROSPERO: My brave spirit!

Who was so firm, so constant, that this coil

Would not infect his reason?

ARIEL: Not a soul

But felt a fever of the mad and play'd

Some tricks of desperation. All but mariners

Plunged in the foaming brine and quit the vessel,

Then all afire with me: the king's son, Ferdinand,

With hair up-staring,-then like reeds, not hair,-

Was the first man that leap'd; cried, 'Hell is

empty

And all the devils are here.'

PROSPERO: Why that's my spirit!

But was not this nigh shore?

ARIEL: Close by, my master.

PROSPERO: But are they, Ariel, safe?

ARIEL: Not a hair perish'd;

On their sustaining garments not a blemish,

But fresher than before: and, as thou badest me,

In troops I have dispersed them 'bout the isle.

The king's son have I landed by himself;

Whom I left cooling of the air with sighs

In an odd angle of the isle and sitting,

His arms in this sad knot.

PROSPERO: Of the king's ship

The mariners say how thou hast disposed

And all the rest o' the fleet.

ARIEL: Safely in harbour

Is the king's ship; in the deep nook, where once

Thou call'dst me up at midnight to fetch dew

From the still-vex'd Bermoothes, there she's hid:

The mariners all under hatches stow'd;

Who, with a charm join'd to their suffer'd labour,

I have left asleep; and for the rest o' the fleet

Which I dispersed, they all have met again

And are upon the Mediterranean flote,

Bound sadly home for Naples,

Supposing that they saw the king's ship wreck'd

And his great person perish.

PROSPERO: Ariel, thy charge

Exactly is perform'd: but there's more work.

What is the time o' the day?

ARIEL: Past the mid season.

PROSPERO: At least two glasses. The time

'twixt six and now

Must by us both be spent most preciously.

ARIEL: Is there more toil? Since thou dost give

me pains,

Let me remember thee what thou hast promised,

Which is not yet perform'd me.

PROSPERO: How now? moody?

What is't thou canst demand?

ARIEL: My liberty.

PROSPERO: Before the time be out? no more!

ARIEL: I prithee,

Remember I have done thee worthy service;

Told thee no lies, made thee no mistakings,

served

Without or grudge or grumblings: thou didst

promise

To bate me a full year.

PROSPERO: Dost thou forget

From what a torment I did free thee?

ARIEL: No.

PROSPERO: Thou dost, and think'st it much to tread the ooze

Of the salt deep,

To run upon the sharp wind of the north,

To do me business in the veins o' the earth

When it is baked with frost.

ARIEL: I do not, sir.

PROSPERO: Thou liest, malignant thing! Hast thou forgot

The foul witch Sycorax, who with age and envy

Was grown into a hoop? hast thou forgot her?

ARIEL: No, sir.

PROSPERO: Thou hast. Where was she born? speak; tell me.

ARIEL: Sir, in Argier.

PROSPERO: O, was she so? I must

Once in a month recount what thou hast been,

Which thou forget'st. This damn'd witch Sycorax,

For mischiefs manifold and sorceries terrible

To enter human hearing, from Argier,

Thou know'st, was banish'd: for one thing she did

They would not take her life. Is not this true?

ARIEL: Ay, sir.

PROSPERO: This blue-eyed hag was hither

brought with child

And here was left by the sailors. Thou, my slave,

As thou report'st thyself, wast then her servant;

And, for thou wast a spirit too delicate

To act her earthy and abhorr'd commands,

Refusing her grand hests, she did confine thee,

By help of her more potent ministers

And in her most unmitigable rage,

Into a cloven pine; within which rift

Imprison'd thou didst painfully remain

A dozen years; within which space she died

And left thee there; where thou didst vent thy

groans

As fast as mill-wheels strike. Then was this

island-

Save for the son that she did litter here,

A freckled whelp hag-born-not honour'd with

A human shape.

ARIEL: Yes, Caliban her son.

PROSPERO: Dull thing, I say so; he, that

Caliban

Whom now I keep in service. Thou best know'st

What torment I did find thee in; thy groans

Did make wolves howl and penetrate the breasts

Of ever angry bears: it was a torment

To lay upon the damn'd, which Sycorax

Could not again undo: it was mine art,

When I arrived and heard thee, that made gape

The pine and let thee out.

ARIEL: I thank thee, master.

PROSPERO: If thou more murmur'st, I will rend an oak

And peg thee in his knotty entrails till

Thou hast howl'd away twelve winters.

ARIEL: Pardon, master;

I will be correspondent to command

And do my spiriting gently.

PROSPERO: Do so, and after two days

I will discharge thee.

ARIEL: That's my noble master!

What shall I do? say what; what shall I do?

PROSPERO: Go make thyself like a nymph o'

the sea: be subject

To no sight but thine and mine, invisible

To every eyeball else. Go take this shape

And hither come in't: go, hence with diligence!

[*Exit ARIEL*]

Awake, dear heart, awake! thou hast slept well;

Awake!

MIRANDA: The strangeness of your story put
Heaviness in me.

PROSPERO: Shake it off. Come on;
We'll visit Caliban my slave, who never
Yields us kind answer.

MIRANDA: 'Tis a villain, sir,
I do not love to look on.

PROSPERO: But, as 'tis,
We cannot miss him: he does make our fire,
Fetch in our wood and serves in offices
That profit us. What, ho! slave! Caliban!
Thou earth, thou! speak.

CALIBAN: [Within] There's wood enough within.

PROSPERO: Come forth, I say! there's other
business for thee:
Come, thou tortoise! when?

[*Re-enter ARIEL like a water-nymph*]

Fine apparition! My quaint Ariel,
Hark in thine ear.

ARIEL: My lord it shall be done.

[*Exit*]

PROSPERO: Thou poisonous slave, got by the
devil himself

Upon thy wicked dam, come forth!

[*Enter CALIBAN*]

CALIBAN: As wicked dew as e'er my mother brush'd

With raven's feather from unwholesome fen

Drop on you both! a south-west blow on ye

And blister you all o'er!

PROSPERO: For this, be sure, to-night thou shalt have cramps,

Side-stitches that shall pen thy breath up; urchins

Shall, for that vast of night that they may work,

All exercise on thee; thou shalt be pinch'd

As thick as honeycomb, each pinch more stinging

Than bees that made 'em.

CALIBAN: I must eat my dinner.

This island's mine, by Sycorax my mother,

Which thou takest from me. When thou camest first,

Thou strokedst me and madest much of me, wouldst give me

Water with berries in't, and teach me how

To name the bigger light, and how the less,

That burn by day and night: and then I loved thee
And show'd thee all the qualities o' the isle,
The fresh springs, brine-pits, barren place and
fertile:
Cursed be I that did so! All the charms
Of Sycorax, toads, beetles, bats, light on you!
For I am all the subjects that you have,
Which first was mine own king: and here you sty
me
In this hard rock, whiles you do keep from me
The rest o' the island.

PROSPERO: Thou most lying slave,
Whom stripes may move, not kindness! I have
used thee,
Filth as thou art, with human care, and lodged
thee
In mine own cell, till thou didst seek to violate
The honour of my child.

CALIBAN: O ho, O ho! would't had been done!
Thou didst prevent me; I had peopled else
This isle with Calibans.

PROSPERO: Abhorred slave,
Which any print of goodness wilt not take,
Being capable of all ill! I pitied thee,

Took pains to make thee speak, taught thee each hour

One thing or other: when thou didst not, savage,

Know thine own meaning, but wouldst gabble like

A thing most brutish, I endow'd thy purposes

With words that made them known. But thy vile race,

Though thou didst learn, had that in't which good natures

Could not abide to be with; therefore wast thou

Deservedly confined into this rock,

Who hadst deserved more than a prison.

CALIBAN: You taught me language; and my profit on't

Is, I know how to curse. The red plague rid you

For learning me your language!

PROSPERO: Hag-seed, hence!

Fetch us in fuel; and be quick, thou'rt best,

To answer other business. Shrug'st thou, malice?

If thou neglect'st or dost unwillingly

What I command, I'll rack thee with old cramps,

Fill all thy bones with aches, make thee roar

That beasts shall tremble at thy din.

CALIBAN: No, pray thee.

[*Aside*]

I must obey: his art is of such power,

It would control my dam's god, Setebos,

and make a vassal of him.

PROSPERO: So, slave; hence!

[*Exit CALIBAN*]

[*Re-enter ARIEL, invisible, playing and singing;
FERDINAND following*]

ARIEL'S song:

Come unto these yellow sands,

And then take hands:

Courtsied when you have and kiss'd

The wild waves whist,

Foot it featly here and there;

And, sweet sprites, the burden bear.

Hark, hark!

[*Burden: dispersedly, within*]

The watch-dogs bark!

[*Burden: Bow-wow*]

Hark, hark! I hear

The strain of strutting chanticleer

[*Cry, Cock-a-diddle-dow.*]

FERDINAND: Where should this music be? i' the air or the earth?

It sounds no more: and sure, it waits upon

Some god o' the island. Sitting on a bank,

Weeping again the king my father's wreck,

This music crept by me upon the waters,

Allaying both their fury and my passion

With its sweet air: thence I have follow'd it,

Or it hath drawn me rather. But 'tis gone.

No, it begins again.

[*ARIEL sings*]

Full fathom five thy father lies;

Of his bones are coral made;

Those are pearls that were his eyes:

Nothing of him that doth fade

But doth suffer a sea-change

Into something rich and strange.

Sea-nymphs hourly ring his knell

[*Burden Ding-dong*]

Hark! now I hear them, Ding-dong, bell.

FERDINAND: The ditty does remember my drown'd father.

This is no mortal business, nor no sound

That the earth owes. I hear it now above me.

PROSPERO: The fringed curtains of thine eye advance

And say what thou seest yond.

MIRANDA: What is't? a spirit?

Lord, how it looks about! Believe me, sir,

It carries a brave form. But 'tis a spirit.

PROSPERO: No, wench; it eats and sleeps and hath such senses

As we have, such. This gallant which thou seest

Was in the wreck; and, but he's something stain'd

With grief that's beauty's canker, thou mightst call him

A goodly person: he hath lost his fellows

And strays about to find 'em.

MIRANDA: I might call him

A thing divine, for nothing natural

I ever saw so noble.

PROSPERO: [Aside] It goes on, I see,

As my soul prompts it. Spirit, fine spirit! I'll free thee

Within two days for this.

FERDINAND: Most sure, the goddess

On whom these airs attend! Vouchsafe my

prayer

May know if you remain upon this island;

And that you will some good instruction give

How I may bear me here: my prime request,

Which I do last pronounce, is, O you wonder!

If you be maid or no?

MIRANDA: No wonder, sir;

But certainly a maid.

FERDINAND: My language! heavens!

I am the best of them that speak this speech,

Were I but where 'tis spoken.

PROSPERO: How? the best?

What wert thou, if the King of Naples heard

thee?

FERDINAND: A single thing, as I am now, that

wonders

To hear thee speak of Naples. He does hear me;

And that he does I weep: myself am Naples,

Who with mine eyes, never since at ebb, beheld

The king my father wreck'd.

MIRANDA: Alack, for mercy!

FERDINAND: Yes, faith, and all his lords; the

Duke of Milan

And his brave son being twain.

PROSPERO: [Aside] The Duke of Milan

And his more braver daughter could control thee,

If now 'twere fit to do't. At the first sight

They have changed eyes. Delicate Ariel,

I'll set thee free for this.

[*To FERDINAND*]

A word, good sir;

I fear you have done yourself some wrong: a

word.

MIRANDA: Why speaks my father so ungently?

This

Is the third man that e'er I saw, the first

That e'er I sigh'd for: pity move my father

To be inclined my way!

FERDINAND: O, if a virgin,

And your affection not gone forth, I'll make you

The queen of Naples.

PROSPERO: Soft, sir! one word more.

[*Aside*]

They are both in either's powers; but this swift

business

I must uneasy make, lest too light winning

Make the prize light.

[*To FERDINAND*]

One word more; I charge thee

That thou attend me: thou dost here usurp

The name thou owest not; and hast put thyself

Upon this island as a spy, to win it

From me, the lord on't.

FERDINAND: No, as I am a man.

MIRANDA: There's nothing ill can dwell in such

a temple:

If the ill spirit have so fair a house,

Good things will strive to dwell with't.

PROSPERO: Follow me.

Speak not you for him; he's a traitor. Come;

I'll manacle thy neck and feet together:

Sea-water shalt thou drink; thy food shall be

The fresh-brook muscles, wither'd roots and

husks

Wherein the acorn cradled. Follow.

FERDINAND: No;

I will resist such entertainment till

Mine enemy has more power.

[*Draws, and is charmed from moving*]

MIRANDA: O dear father,

Make not too rash a trial of him, for

He's gentle and not fearful.

PROSPERO: What? I say,

My foot my tutor? Put thy sword up, traitor;

Who makest a show but darest not strike, thy conscience

Is so possess'd with guilt: come from thy ward,

For I can here disarm thee with this stick

And make thy weapon drop.

MIRANDA: Beseech you, father.

PROSPERO: Hence! hang not on my garments.

MIRANDA: Sir, have pity;

I'll be his surety.

PROSPERO: Silence! one word more

Shall make me chide thee, if not hate thee.

What!

An advocate for an imposter! hush!

Thou think'st there is no more such shapes as he,

Having seen but him and Caliban: foolish wench!

To the most of men this is a Caliban

And they to him are angels.

MIRANDA: My affections

Are then most humble; I have no ambition

To see a goodlier man.

PROSPERO: Come on; obey:

Thy nerves are in their infancy again

And have no vigour in them.

FERDINAND: So they are;

My spirits, as in a dream, are all bound up.

My father's loss, the weakness which I feel,

The wreck of all my friends, nor this man's

threats,

To whom I am subdued, are but light to me,

Might I but through my prison once a day

Behold this maid: all corners else o' the earth

Let liberty make use of; space enough

Have I in such a prison.

PROSPERO: [Aside] It works.

[*To FERDINAND*]

Come on.

Thou hast done well, fine Ariel!

[*To FERDINAND*]

Follow me.

[*To ARIEL*]

Hark what thou else shalt do me.

MIRANDA: Be of comfort;

My father's of a better nature, sir,

Than he appears by speech: this is unwonted

Which now came from him.

PROSPERO: Thou shalt be free

As mountain winds: but then exactly do

All points of my command.

ARIEL: To the syllable.

PROSPERO: Come, follow. Speak not for him.

[*Exeunt*]

My Notes

ACT II

SCENE I – Another part of the island.

[*Enter ALONSO, SEBASTIAN, ANTONIO, GONZALO, ADRIAN, FRANCISCO, and others*]

GONZALO: Beseech you, sir, be merry; you have cause,

So have we all, of joy; for our escape

Is much beyond our loss. Our hint of woe

Is common; every day some sailor's wife,

The masters of some merchant and the merchant

Have just our theme of woe; but for the miracle,

I mean our preservation, few in millions

Can speak like us: then wisely, good sir, weigh

Our sorrow with our comfort.

ALONSO: Prithee, peace.

SEBASTIAN: He receives comfort like cold porridge.

ANTONIO: The visitor will not give him o'er so.

SEBASTIAN: Look he's winding up the watch of his wit;

by and by it will strike.

GONZALO: Sir,-

SEBASTIAN: One: tell.

GONZALO: When every grief is entertain'd that's offer'd,

Comes to the entertainer-

SEBASTIAN: A dollar.

GONZALO: Dolour comes to him, indeed: you have spoken truer than you purposed.

SEBASTIAN: You have taken it wiselier than I meant you should.

GONZALO: Therefore, my lord,-

ANTONIO: Fie, what a spendthrift is he of his tongue!

ALONSO: I prithee, spare.

GONZALO: Well, I have done: but yet,-

SEBASTIAN: He will be talking.

ANTONIO: Which, of he or Adrian, for a good wager, first begins to crow?

SEBASTIAN: The old cock.

ANTONIO: The cockerel.

SEBASTIAN: Done. The wager?

ANTONIO: A laughter.

SEBASTIAN: A match!

ADRIAN: Though this island seem to be desert,-

SEBASTIAN: Ha, ha, ha! So, you're paid.

ADRIAN: Uninhabitable and almost inaccessible,-

SEBASTIAN: Yet,-

ADRIAN: Yet,-

ANTONIO: He could not miss't.

ADRIAN: It must needs be of subtle, tender and delicate temperance.

ANTONIO: Temperance was a delicate wench.

SEBASTIAN: Ay, and a subtle; as he most learnedly delivered.

ADRIAN: The air breathes upon us here most sweetly.

SEBASTIAN: As if it had lungs and rotten ones.

ANTONIO: Or as 'twere perfumed by a fen.

GONZALO: Here is everything advantageous to life.

ANTONIO: True; save means to live.

SEBASTIAN: Of that there's none, or little.

GONZALO: How lush and lusty the grass looks! how green!

ANTONIO: The ground indeed is tawny.

SEBASTIAN: With an eye of green in't.

ANTONIO: He misses not much.

SEBASTIAN: No; he doth but mistake the truth totally.

GONZALO: But the rarity of it is,-which is indeed almost beyond credit,-

SEBASTIAN: As many vouched rarities are.

GONZALO: That our garments, being, as they were, drenched in the sea, hold notwithstanding their freshness and glosses, being rather new-dyed than stained with salt water.

ANTONIO: If but one of his pockets could speak, would it not say he lies?

SEBASTIAN: Ay, or very falsely pocket up his report.

GONZALO: Methinks our garments are now as fresh as when we put them on first in Afric, at the marriage of the king's fair daughter Claribel to the King of Tunis.

SEBASTIAN: 'Twas a sweet marriage, and we prosper well in our return.

ADRIAN: Tunis was never graced before with such a paragon to their queen.

GONZALO: Not since widow Dido's time.

ANTONIO: Widow! a pox o' that! How came that widow in? widow Dido!

SEBASTIAN: What if he had said 'widower Aeneas' too? Good Lord, how you take it!

ADRIAN: 'Widow Dido' said you? you make me study of that: she was of Carthage, not of Tunis.

GONZALO: This Tunis, sir, was Carthage.

ADRIAN: Carthage?

GONZALO: I assure you, Carthage.

SEBASTIAN: His word is more than the miraculous harp; he hath raised the wall and houses too.

ANTONIO: What impossible matter will he make easy next?

SEBASTIAN: I think he will carry this island home in his pocket and give it his son for an apple.

ANTONIO: And, sowing the kernels of it in the sea, bring forth more islands.

GONZALO: Ay.

ANTONIO: Why, in good time.

GONZALO: Sir, we were talking that our garments seem now as fresh as when we were at Tunis at the marriage of your daughter, who is now queen.

ANTONIO: And the rarest that e'er came there.

SEBASTIAN: Bate, I beseech you, widow Dido.

ANTONIO: O, widow Dido! ay, widow Dido.

GONZALO: Is not, sir, my doublet as fresh as
the first day I wore it? I mean, in a sort.

ANTONIO: That sort was well fished for.

GONZALO: When I wore it at your daughter's
marriage?

ALONSO: You cram these words into mine ears
against
The stomach of my sense. Would I had never
Married my daughter there! for, coming thence,
My son is lost and, in my rate, she too,
Who is so far from Italy removed
I ne'er again shall see her. O thou mine heir
Of Naples and of Milan, what strange fish
Hath made his meal on thee?

FRANCISCO: Sir, he may live:
I saw him beat the surges under him,
And ride upon their backs; he trod the water,
Whose enmity he flung aside, and breasted
The surge most swoln that met him; his bold
head
'Bove the contentious waves he kept, and oar'd
Himself with his good arms in lusty stroke

To the shore, that o'er his wave-worn basis
bow'd,
As stooping to relieve him: I not doubt
He came alive to land.

ALONSO: No, no, he's gone.

SEBASTIAN: Sir, you may thank yourself for this
great loss,
That would not bless our Europe with your
daughter,
But rather lose her to an African;
Where she at least is banish'd from your eye,
Who hath cause to wet the grief on't.

ALONSO: Prithee, peace.

SEBASTIAN: You were kneel'd to and
importuned otherwise
By all of us, and the fair soul herself
Weigh'd between loathness and obedience, at
Which end o' the beam should bow. We have
lost your son,
I fear, for ever: Milan and Naples have
More widows in them of this business' making
Than we bring men to comfort them:
The fault's your own.

ALONSO: So is the dear'st o' the loss.

GONZALO: My lord Sebastian,

The truth you speak doth lack some gentleness

And time to speak it in: you rub the sore,

When you should bring the plaster.

SEBASTIAN: Very well.

ANTONIO: And most chirurgeonly.

GONZALO: It is foul weather in us all, good sir,

When you are cloudy.

SEBASTIAN: Foul weather?

ANTONIO: Very foul.

GONZALO: Had I plantation of this isle, my lord,-

ANTONIO: He'ld sow't with nettle-seed.

SEBASTIAN: Or docks, or mallows.

GONZALO: And were the king on't, what would I do?

SEBASTIAN: 'Scape being drunk for want of wine.

GONZALO: I' the commonwealth I would by contraries

Execute all things; for no kind of traffic

Would I admit; no name of magistrate;

Letters should not be known; riches, poverty,

And use of service, none; contract, succession,

Bourn, bound of land, tilth, vineyard, none;

No use of metal, corn, or wine, or oil;

No occupation; all men idle, all;

And women too, but innocent and pure;

No sovereignty;-

SEBASTIAN: Yet he would be king on't.

ANTONIO: The latter end of his commonwealth

forgets the beginning.

GONZALO: All things in common nature should

produce

Without sweat or endeavour: treason, felony,

Sword, pike, knife, gun, or need of any engine,

Would I not have; but nature should bring forth,

Of its own kind, all foison, all abundance,

To feed my innocent people.

SEBASTIAN: No marrying 'mong his subjects?

ANTONIO: None, man; all idle: whores and

knaves.

GONZALO: I would with such perfection govern,

sir,

To excel the golden age.

SEBASTIAN: God save his majesty!

ANTONIO: Long live Gonzalo!

GONZALO: And,-do you mark me, sir?

ALONSO: Prithee, no more: thou dost talk

nothing to me.

GONZALO: I do well believe your highness; and did it to minister occasion to these gentlemen, who are of such sensible and nimble lungs that they always use to laugh at nothing.

ANTONIO: 'Twas you we laughed at.

GONZALO: Who in this kind of merry fooling am nothing to you: so you may continue and laugh at nothing still.

ANTONIO: What a blow was there given!

SEBASTIAN: An it had not fallen flat-long.

GONZALO: You are gentlemen of brave metal; you would lift the moon out of her sphere, if she would continue in it five weeks without changing.

[*Enter ARIEL, invisible, playing solemn music*]

SEBASTIAN: We would so, and then go a bat-fowling.

ANTONIO: Nay, good my lord, be not angry.

GONZALO: No, I warrant you; I will not adventure my discretion so weakly. Will you laugh me asleep, for I am very heavy?

ANTONIO: Go sleep, and hear us.

[*All sleep except ALONSO, SEBASTIAN, and ANTONIO*]

ALONSO: What, all so soon asleep! I wish mine eyes

Would, with themselves, shut up my thoughts: I find

They are inclined to do so.

SEBASTIAN: Please you, sir,

Do not omit the heavy offer of it:

It seldom visits sorrow; when it doth,

It is a comforter.

ANTONIO: We two, my lord,

Will guard your person while you take your rest,

And watch your safety.

ALONSO: Thank you. Wondrous heavy.

[*ALONSO sleeps. Exit ARIEL*]

SEBASTIAN: What a strange drowsiness possesses them!

ANTONIO: It is the quality o' the climate.

SEBASTIAN: Why

Doth it not then our eyelids sink? I find not

Myself disposed to sleep.

ANTONIO: Nor I; my spirits are nimble.

They fell together all, as by consent;

They dropp'd, as by a thunder-stroke. What might,

Worthy Sebastian? O, what might? No more:
And yet me thinks I see it in thy face,
What thou shouldst be: the occasion speaks
thee, and
My strong imagination sees a crown
Dropping upon thy head.

SEBASTIAN: What, art thou waking?

ANTONIO: Do you not hear me speak?

SEBASTIAN: I do; and surely
It is a sleepy language and thou speak'st
Out of thy sleep. What is it thou didst say?
This is a strange repose, to be asleep
With eyes wide open; standing, speaking,
moving,
And yet so fast asleep.

ANTONIO: Noble Sebastian,
Thou let'st thy fortune sleep-die, rather; wink'st
Whiles thou art waking.

SEBASTIAN: Thou dost snore distinctly;
There's meaning in thy snores.

ANTONIO: I am more serious than my custom:
you
Must be so too, if heed me; which to do
Trebles thee o'er.

SEBASTIAN: Well, I am standing water.

ANTONIO: I'll teach you how to flow.

SEBASTIAN: Do so: to ebb

Hereditary sloth instructs me.

ANTONIO: O!

If you but knew how you the purpose cherish

Whiles thus you mock it! how, in stripping it,

You more invest it! Ebbing men, indeed,

Most often do so near the bottom run

By their own fear or sloth.

SEBASTIAN: Prithee, say on:

The setting of thine eye and cheek proclaim

A matter from thee, and a birth indeed

Which throes thee much to yield.

ANTONIO: Thus, sir:

Although this lord of weak remembrance, this,

Who shall be of as little memory

When he is earth'd, hath here almost persuade,

For he's a spirit of persuasion, only

Professes to persuade, the king his son's alive,

'Tis as impossible that he's undrown'd

And he that sleeps here swims.

SEBASTIAN: I have no hope

That he's undrown'd.

ANTONIO: O, out of that 'no hope'

What great hope have you! no hope that way is

Another way so high a hope that even

Ambition cannot pierce a wink beyond,

But doubt discovery there. Will you grant with me

That Ferdinand is drown'd?

SEBASTIAN: He's gone.

ANTONIO: Then, tell me,

Who's the next heir of Naples?

SEBASTIAN: Claribel.

ANTONIO: She that is queen of Tunis; she that dwells

Ten leagues beyond man's life; she that from Naples

Can have no note, unless the sun were post-

The man i' the moon's too slow, till new-born chins

Be rough and razorable; she that, from whom?

We all were sea-swallow'd, though some cast again,

And by that destiny to perform an act

Whereof what's past is prologue, what to come

In yours and my discharge.

SEBASTIAN: What stuff is this! how say you?

'Tis true, my brother's daughter's queen of Tunis;

So is she heir of Naples; 'twixt which regions

There is some space.

ANTONIO: A space whose every cubit

Seems to cry out, 'How shall that Claribel

Measure us back to Naples? Keep in Tunis,

And let Sebastian wake.' Say, this were death

That now hath seized them; why, they were no worse

Than now they are. There be that can rule Naples

As well as he that sleeps; lords that can prate

As amply and unnecessarily

As this Gonzalo; I myself could make

A chough of as deep chat. O, that you bore

The mind that I do! what a sleep were this

For your advancement! Do you understand me?

SEBASTIAN: Methinks I do.

ANTONIO: And how does your content

Tender your own good fortune?

SEBASTIAN: I remember

You did supplant your brother Prospero.

ANTONIO: True:

And look how well my garments sit upon me;

Much feater than before: my brother's servants

Were then my fellows; now they are my men.

SEBASTIAN: But, for your conscience?

ANTONIO: Ay, sir; where lies that? if 'twere a kibe,

'Twould put me to my slipper: but I feel not

This deity in my bosom: twenty consciences,

That stand 'twixt me and Milan, candied be they

And melt ere they molest! Here lies your brother,

No better than the earth he lies upon,

If he were that which now he's like, that's dead;

Whom I, with this obedient steel, three inches of it,

Can lay to bed for ever; whiles you, doing thus,

To the perpetual wink for aye might put

This ancient morsel, this Sir Prudence, who

Should not upbraid our course. For all the rest,

They'll take suggestion as a cat laps milk;

They'll tell the clock to any business that

We say befits the hour.

SEBASTIAN: Thy case, dear friend,

Shall be my precedent; as thou got'st Milan,

I'll come by Naples. Draw thy sword: one stroke

Shall free thee from the tribute which thou

payest;

And I the king shall love thee.

ANTONIO: Draw together;

And when I rear my hand, do you the like,

To fall it on Gonzalo.

SEBASTIAN: O, but one word.

[*They talk apart*]

[*Re-enter ARIEL, invisible*]

ARIEL: My master through his art foresees the danger

That you, his friend, are in; and sends me forth-

For else his project dies-to keep them living.

[*Sings in GONZALO's ear*]

While you here do snoring lie,

Open-eyed conspiracy

His time doth take.

If of life you keep a care,

Shake off slumber, and beware:

Awake, awake!

ANTONIO: Then let us both be sudden.

GONZALO: Now, good angels

Preserve the king.

[*They wake*]

ALONSO: Why, how now? ho, awake! Why are

you drawn?

Wherefore this ghastly looking?

GONZALO: What's the matter?

SEBASTIAN: Whiles we stood here securing
your repose,

Even now, we heard a hollow burst of bellowing

Like bulls, or rather lions: did't not wake you?

It struck mine ear most terribly.

ALONSO: I heard nothing.

ANTONIO: O, 'twas a din to fright a monster's
ear,

To make an earthquake! sure, it was the roar

Of a whole herd of lions.

ALONSO: Heard you this, Gonzalo?

GONZALO: Upon mine honour, sir, I heard a
humming,

And that a strange one too, which did awake me:

I shaked you, sir, and cried: as mine eyes
open'd,

I saw their weapons drawn: there was a noise,

That's verily. 'Tis best we stand upon our guard,

Or that we quit this place; let's draw our
weapons.

ALONSO: Lead off this ground; and let's make

further search

For my poor son.

GONZALO: Heavens keep him from these

beasts!

For he is, sure, i' the island.

ALONSO: Lead away.

ARIEL: Prospero my lord shall know what I have

done:

So, king, go safely on to seek thy son.

[*Exeunt*]

SCENE II – Another part of the island.

[*Enter CALIBAN with a burden of wood. A noise
of thunder heard*]

CALIBAN: All the infections that the sun sucks

up

From bogs, fens, flats, on Prosper fall and make

him

By inch-meal a disease! His spirits hear me

And yet I needs must curse. But they'll nor pinch,

Fright me with urchin-shows, pitch me i' the mire,

Nor lead me, like a firebrand, in the dark

Out of my way, unless he bid 'em; but

For every trifle are they set upon me;
Sometime like apes that mow and chatter at me
And after bite me, then like hedgehogs which
Lie tumbling in my barefoot way and mount
Their pricks at my footfall; sometime am I
All wound with adders who with cloven tongues
Do hiss me into madness.
[*Enter TRINCULO*]
Lo, now, lo!
Here comes a spirit of his, and to torment me
For bringing wood in slowly. I'll fall flat;
Perchance he will not mind me.

TRINCULO: Here's neither bush nor shrub, to bear off any weather at all, and another storm brewing; I hear it sing i' the wind: yond same black cloud, yond huge one, looks like a foul bombard that would shed his liquor. If it should thunder as it did before, I know not where to hide my head: yond same cloud cannot choose but fall by pailfuls. What have we here? a man or a fish? dead or alive? A fish: he smells like a fish; a very ancient and fish-like smell; a kind of not of the newest Poor-John. A strange fish! Were I in England now, as once I was, and had but this

fish painted, not a holiday fool there but would give a piece of silver: there would this monster make a man; any strange beast there makes a man:
when they will not give a doit to relieve a lame beggar, they will lazy out ten to see a dead Indian. Legged like a man and his fins like arms! Warm o' my troth! I do now let loose my opinion; hold it no longer: this is no fish, but an islander, that hath lately suffered by a thunderbolt.
[*Thunder*]
Alas, the storm is come again! my best way is to creep under his gaberdine; there is no other shelter hereabouts: misery acquaints a man with strange bed-fellows. I will here shroud till the dregs of the storm be past.
[*Enter STEPHANO, singing: a bottle in his hand*]
STEPHANO: *I shall no more to sea, to sea,*
Here shall I die ashore-
This is a very scurvy tune to sing at a man's funeral: well, here's my comfort.
[*Drinks*]
[*Sings*]
The master, the swabber, the boatswain and I,

The gunner and his mate

Loved Mall, Meg and Marian and Margery,

But none of us cared for Kate;

For she had a tongue with a tang,

Would cry to a sailor, Go hang!

She loved not the savour of tar nor of pitch,

Yet a tailor might scratch her where'er she did

itch:

Then to sea, boys, and let her go hang!

This is a scurvy tune too: but here's my comfort.
[*Drinks*]

CALIBAN: Do not torment me: Oh!

STEPHANO: What's the matter? Have we devils
here? Do you put tricks upon's with savages and
men of Ind, ha? I have not scaped drowning to
be afeard now of your four legs; for it hath been
said, As proper a man as ever went on four legs
cannot make him give ground; and it shall be
said so again while Stephano breathes at's
nostrils.

CALIBAN: The spirit torments me; Oh!

STEPHANO: This is some monster of the isle
with four legs, who hath got, as I take it, an ague.
Where the devil should he learn our language? I

will give him some relief, if it be but for that. if I can recover him and keep him tame and get to Naples with him, he's a present for any emperor that ever trod on neat's leather.

CALIBAN: Do not torment me, prithee; I'll bring my wood home faster.

STEPHANO: He's in his fit now and does not talk after the wisest. He shall taste of my bottle: if he have never drunk wine afore will go near to remove his fit. If I can recover him and keep him tame, I will not take too much for him; he shall pay for him that hath him, and that soundly.

CALIBAN: Thou dost me yet but little hurt; thou wilt anon, I know it by thy trembling: now Prosper works upon thee.

STEPHANO: Come on your ways; open your mouth; here is that which will give language to you, cat: open your mouth; this will shake your shaking, I can tell you, and that soundly: you cannot tell who's your friend: open your chaps again.

TRINCULO: I should know that voice: it should be, but he is drowned; and these are devils: O defend me!

STEPHANO: Four legs and two voices: a most delicate monster! His forward voice now is to speak well of his friend; his backward voice is to utter foul speeches and to detract. If all the wine in my bottle will recover him, I will help his ague. Come. Amen! I will pour some in thy other mouth.

TRINCULO: Stephano!

STEPHANO: Doth thy other mouth call me? Mercy, mercy! This is a devil, and no monster: I will leave him; I have no long spoon.

TRINCULO: Stephano! If thou beest Stephano, touch me and speak to me: for I am Trinculo, be not afeard, thy good friend Trinculo.

STEPHANO: If thou beest Trinculo, come forth: I'll pull thee by the lesser legs: if any be Trinculo's legs, these are they. Thou art very Trinculo indeed! How camest thou to be the siege of this moon-calf? Can he vent Trinculos?

TRINCULO: I took him to be killed with a thunder-stroke. But art thou not drowned, Stephano? I hope now thou art not drowned. Is the storm overblown? I hid me under the dead moon-calf's gaberdine for fear of the storm. And art thou living, Stephano? O Stephano, two Neapolitans 'scaped!

STEPHANO: Prithee, do not turn me about; my stomach is not constant.

CALIBAN: [Aside] These be fine things, an if they be not sprites.
That's a brave god and bears celestial liquor.
I will kneel to him.

STEPHANO: How didst thou 'scape? How camest thou hither? swear by this bottle how thou camest hither. I escaped upon a butt of sack which the sailors heaved o'erboard, by this bottle; which I made of the bark of a tree with mine own hands since I was cast ashore.

CALIBAN: I'll swear upon that bottle to be thy true subject; for the liquor is not earthly.

STEPHANO: Here; swear then how thou escapedst.

TRINCULO: Swum ashore. man, like a duck: I can swim like a duck, I'll be sworn.

STEPHANO: Here, kiss the book. Though thou canst swim like a duck, thou art made like a goose.

TRINCULO: O Stephano. hast any more of this?

STEPHANO: The whole butt, man: my cellar is in a rock by the sea-side where my wine is hid. How now, moon-calf! how does thine ague?

CALIBAN: Hast thou not dropp'd from heaven?

STEPHANO: Out o' the moon, I do assure thee: I was the man i' the moon when time was.

CALIBAN: I have seen thee in her and I do adore thee:

My mistress show'd me thee and thy dog and thy bush.

STEPHANO: Come, swear to that; kiss the book: I will furnish it anon with new contents swear.

TRINCULO: By this good light, this is a very shallow monster! I afeard of him! A very weak monster! The man i' the moon! A most poor credulous monster! Well

drawn, monster, in good sooth!

CALIBAN: I'll show thee every fertile inch o' th' island;

And I will kiss thy foot: I prithee, be my god.

TRINCULO: By this light, a most perfidious and drunken monster! when 's god's asleep, he'll rob his bottle.

CALIBAN: I'll kiss thy foot; I'll swear myself thy subject.

STEPHANO: Come on then; down, and swear.

TRINCULO: I shall laugh myself to death at this puppy-headed monster. A most scurvy monster! I could find in my heart to beat him,-

STEPHANO: Come, kiss.

TRINCULO: But that the poor monster's in drink: an abominable monster!

CALIBAN: I'll show thee the best springs; I'll pluck thee berries;

I'll fish for thee and get thee wood enough.

A plague upon the tyrant that I serve!

I'll bear him no more sticks, but follow thee,

Thou wondrous man.

TRINCULO: A most ridiculous monster, to make a wonder of a poor drunkard!

CALIBAN: I prithee, let me bring thee where crabs grow;

And I with my long nails will dig thee pignuts;

Show thee a jay's nest and instruct thee how

To snare the nimble marmoset; I'll bring thee

To clustering filberts and sometimes I'll get thee

Young scamels from the rock. Wilt thou go with

me?

STEPHANO: I prithee now, lead the way without any more talking. Trinculo, the king and all our company else being drowned, we will inherit here: here; bear my bottle: fellow Trinculo, we'll fill him by and by again.

CALIBAN: [Sings drunkenly]

Farewell master; farewell, farewell!

TRINCULO: A howling monster: a drunken monster!

CALIBAN: *No more dams I'll make for fish;*

Nor fetch in firing

At requiring;

Nor scrape trencher, nor wash dish

'Ban, 'Ban, Ca-Caliban

Has a new master: get a new man.

Freedom, hey-day! hey-day, freedom! freedom, hey-day, freedom!

STEPHANO: O brave monster! Lead the way.

[*Exeunt*]

My Notes

ACT III

SCENE I – Before Prospero's Cell.

[*Enter FERDINAND, bearing a log*]

FERDINAND: There be some sports are painful,
and their labour

Delight in them sets off: some kinds of baseness

Are nobly undergone and most poor matters

Point to rich ends. This my mean task

Would be as heavy to me as odious, but

The mistress which I serve quickens what's dead

And makes my labours pleasures: O, she is

Ten times more gentle than her father's crabbed,

And he's composed of harshness. I must remove

Some thousands of these logs and pile them up,

Upon a sore injunction: my sweet mistress

Weeps when she sees me work, and says, such
baseness

Had never like executor. I forget:

But these sweet thoughts do even refresh my
labours,

Most busy lest, when I do it.

[*Enter MIRANDA; and PROSPERO at a*

distance, unseen]

MIRANDA: Alas, now, pray you,

Work not so hard: I would the lightning had

Burnt up those logs that you are enjoin'd to pile!

Pray, set it down and rest you: when this burns,

'Twill weep for having wearied you. My father

Is hard at study; pray now, rest yourself;

He's safe for these three hours.

FERDINAND: O most dear mistress,

The sun will set before I shall discharge

What I must strive to do.

MIRANDA: If you'll sit down,

I'll bear your logs the while: pray, give me that;

I'll carry it to the pile.

FERDINAND: No, precious creature;

I had rather crack my sinews, break my back,

Than you should such dishonour undergo,

While I sit lazy by.

MIRANDA: It would become me

As well as it does you: and I should do it

With much more ease; for my good will is to it,

And yours it is against.

PROSPERO: Poor worm, thou art infected!

This visitation shows it.

MIRANDA: You look wearily.

FERDINAND: No, noble mistress; 'tis fresh
morning with me
When you are by at night. I do beseech you-
Chiefly that I might set it in my prayers-
What is your name?

MIRANDA: Miranda.-O my father,
I have broke your hest to say so!

FERDINAND: Admired Miranda!
Indeed the top of admiration! worth
What's dearest to the world! Full many a lady
I have eyed with best regard and many a time
The harmony of their tongues hath into bondage
Brought my too diligent ear: for several virtues
Have I liked several women; never any
With so fun soul, but some defect in her
Did quarrel with the noblest grace she owed
And put it to the foil: but you, O you,
So perfect and so peerless, are created
Of every creature's best!

MIRANDA: I do not know
One of my sex; no woman's face remember,
Save, from my glass, mine own; nor have I seen
More that I may call men than you, good friend,

And my dear father: how features are abroad,

I am skilless of; but, by my modesty,

The jewel in my dower, I would not wish

Any companion in the world but you,

Nor can imagination form a shape,

Besides yourself, to like of. But I prattle

Something too wildly and my father's precepts

I therein do forget.

FERDINAND: I am in my condition

A prince, Miranda; I do think, a king;

I would, not so!-and would no more endure

This wooden slavery than to suffer

The flesh-fly blow my mouth. Hear my soul

speak:

The very instant that I saw you, did

My heart fly to your service; there resides,

To make me slave to it; and for your sake

Am I this patient log-man.

MIRANDA: Do you love me?

FERDINAND: O heaven, O earth, bear witness

to this sound

And crown what I profess with kind event

If I speak true! if hollowly, invert

What best is boded me to mischief! I

Beyond all limit of what else i' the world

Do love, prize, honour you.

MIRANDA: I am a fool

To weep at what I am glad of.

PROSPERO: Fair encounter

Of two most rare affections! Heavens rain grace

On that which breeds between 'em!

FERDINAND: Wherefore weep you?

MIRANDA: At mine unworthiness that dare not offer

What I desire to give, and much less take

What I shall die to want. But this is trifling;

And all the more it seeks to hide itself,

The bigger bulk it shows. Hence, bashful cunning!

And prompt me, plain and holy innocence!

I am your wife, if you will marry me;

If not, I'll die your maid: to be your fellow

You may deny me; but I'll be your servant,

Whether you will or no.

FERDINAND: My mistress, dearest;

And I thus humble ever.

MIRANDA: My husband, then?

FERDINAND: Ay, with a heart as willing

As bondage e'er of freedom: here's my hand.

MIRANDA: And mine, with my heart in't; and now farewell

Till half an hour hence.

FERDINAND: A thousand thousand!

[*Exeunt FERDINAND and MIRANDA severally*]

PROSPERO: So glad of this as they I cannot be,

Who are surprised withal; but my rejoicing

At nothing can be more. I'll to my book,

For yet ere supper-time must I perform

Much business appertaining.

[*Exit*]

SCENE II – Another part of the island.

[*Enter CALIBAN, STEPHANO, and TRINCULO*]

STEPHANO: Tell not me; when the butt is out, we will drink water; not a drop before: therefore bear up, and board 'em. Servant-monster, drink to me.

TRINCULO: Servant-monster! the folly of this island! They say there's but five upon this isle: we are three of them; if th' other two be brained like us, the state totters.

STEPHANO: Drink, servant-monster, when I bid thee: thy eyes are almost set in thy head.

TRINCULO: Where should they be set else? he were a brave monster indeed, if they were set in his tail.

STEPHANO: My man-monster hath drown'd his tongue in sack: for my part, the sea cannot drown me; I swam, ere I could recover the shore, five and thirty leagues off and on. By this light, thou shalt be my lieutenant, monster, or my standard.

TRINCULO: Your lieutenant, if you list; he's no standard.

STEPHANO: We'll not run, Monsieur Monster.

TRINCULO: Nor go neither; but you'll lie like dogs and yet say nothing neither.

STEPHANO: Moon-calf, speak once in thy life, if thou beest a good moon-calf.

CALIBAN: How does thy honour? Let me lick thy shoe.

I'll not serve him; he's not valiant.

TRINCULO: Thou liest, most ignorant monster: I am in case to justle a constable. Why, thou deboshed fish thou, was there ever man a

coward that hath drunk so much sack as I to-
day? Wilt thou tell a monstrous lie, being but half
a fish and half a monster?

CALIBAN: Lo, how he mocks me! wilt thou let
him, my lord?

TRINCULO: 'Lord' quoth he! That a monster
should be such a natural!

CALIBAN: Lo, lo, again! bite him to death, I
prithee.

STEPHANO: Trinculo, keep a good tongue in
your head: if you prove a mutineer,-the next tree!
The poor monster's my subject and he shall not
suffer indignity.

CALIBAN: I thank my noble lord. Wilt thou be
pleased to hearken once again to the suit I made
to thee?

STEPHANO: Marry, will I kneel and repeat it; I
will stand, and so shall Trinculo.

[Enter ARIEL, invisible]

CALIBAN: As I told thee before, I am subject to
a tyrant, a sorcerer, that by his cunning hath
cheated me of the island.

ARIEL: Thou liest.

CALIBAN: Thou liest, thou jesting monkey, thou:

I would my valiant master would destroy thee! I do not lie.

STEPHANO: Trinculo, if you trouble him any more in's tale, by this hand, I will supplant some of your teeth.

TRINCULO: Why, I said nothing.

STEPHANO: Mum, then, and no more. Proceed.

CALIBAN: I say, by sorcery he got this isle;
From me he got it. if thy greatness will
Revenge it on him,-for I know thou darest,
But this thing dare not,-

STEPHANO: That's most certain.

CALIBAN: Thou shalt be lord of it and I'll serve thee.

STEPHANO: How now shall this be compassed?
Canst thou bring me to the party?

CALIBAN: Yea, yea, my lord: I'll yield him thee asleep,
Where thou mayst knock a nail into his bead.

ARIEL: Thou liest; thou canst not.

CALIBAN: What a pied ninny's this! Thou scurvy patch!
I do beseech thy greatness, give him blows
And take his bottle from him: when that's gone

He shall drink nought but brine; for I'll not show him

Where the quick freshes are.

STEPHANO: Trinculo, run into no further danger: interrupt the monster one word further, and, by this hand, I'll turn my mercy out o' doors and make a stock-fish of thee.

TRINCULO: Why, what did I? I did nothing. I'll go farther off.

STEPHANO: Didst thou not say he lied?

ARIEL: Thou liest.

STEPHANO: Do I so? take thou that.

[*Beats TRINCULO*]

As you like this, give me the lie another time.

TRINCULO: I did not give the lie. Out o' your wits and bearing too? A pox o' your bottle! this can sack and drinking do. A murrain on your monster, and the devil take your fingers!

CALIBAN: Ha, ha, ha!

STEPHANO: Now, forward with your tale. Prithee, stand farther off.

CALIBAN: Beat him enough: after a little time I'll beat him too.

STEPHANO: Stand farther. Come, proceed.

CALIBAN: Why, as I told thee, 'tis a custom with him,

I' th' afternoon to sleep: there thou mayst brain him,

Having first seized his books, or with a log

Batter his skull, or paunch him with a stake,

Or cut his wezand with thy knife. Remember

First to possess his books; for without them

He's but a sot, as I am, nor hath not

One spirit to command: they all do hate him

As rootedly as I. Burn but his books.

He has brave utensils,-for so he calls them-

Which when he has a house, he'll deck withal

And that most deeply to consider is

The beauty of his daughter; he himself

Calls her a nonpareil: I never saw a woman,

But only Sycorax my dam and she;

But she as far surpasseth Sycorax

As great'st does least.

STEPHANO: Is it so brave a lass?

CALIBAN: Ay, lord; she will become thy bed, I warrant.

And bring thee forth brave brood.

STEPHANO: Monster, I will kill this man: his

daughter and I will be king and queen-save our graces! and Trinculo and thyself shall be viceroys. Dost thou like the plot, Trinculo?

TRINCULO: Excellent.

STEPHANO: Give me thy hand: I am sorry I beat thee; but, while thou livest, keep a good tongue in thy head.

CALIBAN: Within this half hour will he be asleep:

Wilt thou destroy him then?

STEPHANO: Ay, on mine honour.

ARIEL: This will I tell my master.

CALIBAN: Thou makest me merry; I am full of pleasure:

Let us be jocund: will you troll the catch

You taught me but while-ere?

STEPHANO: At thy request, monster, I will do reason, any reason. Come on, Trinculo, let us sing.

[*Sings*]

Flout 'em and scout 'em

And scout 'em and flout 'em

Thought is free.

CALIBAN: That's not the tune.

[*Ariel plays the tune on a tabour and pipe*]

STEPHANO: What is this same?

TRINCULO: This is the tune of our catch, played by the picture of Nobody.

STEPHANO: If thou beest a man, show thyself in thy likeness: if thou beest a devil, take't as thou list.

TRINCULO: O, forgive me my sins!

STEPHANO: He that dies pays all debts: I defy thee. Mercy upon us!

CALIBAN: Art thou afeard?

STEPHANO: No, monster, not I.

CALIBAN: Be not afeard; the isle is full of noises,

Sounds and sweet airs, that give delight and hurt not.

Sometimes a thousand twangling instruments

Will hum about mine ears, and sometime voices

That, if I then had waked after long sleep,

Will make me sleep again: and then, in dreaming,

The clouds methought would open and show riches

Ready to drop upon me that, when I waked,

I cried to dream again.

STEPHANO: This will prove a brave kingdom to me, where I shall have my music for nothing.

CALIBAN: When Prospero is destroyed.

STEPHANO: That shall be by and by: I remember the story.

TRINCULO: The sound is going away; let's follow it, and after do our work.

STEPHANO: Lead, monster; we'll follow. I would I could see this tabourer; he lays it on.

TRINCULO: Wilt come? I'll follow, Stephano.

[*Exeunt*]

SCENE III – Another part of the island.

[*Enter ALONSO, SEBASTIAN, ANTONIO, GONZALO, ADRIAN, FRANCISCO, and others*]

GONZALO: By'r lakin, I can go no further, sir;
My old bones ache: here's a maze trod indeed
Through forth-rights and meanders! By your patience,
I needs must rest me.

ALONSO: Old lord, I cannot blame thee,
Who am myself attach'd with weariness,

To the dulling of my spirits: sit down, and rest.
Even here I will put off my hope and keep it
No longer for my flatterer: he is drown'd
Whom thus we stray to find, and the sea mocks
Our frustrate search on land. Well, let him go.

ANTONIO: [Aside to SEBASTIAN] I am right glad that he's so out of hope.
Do not, for one repulse, forego the purpose
That you resolved to effect.

SEBASTIAN: [Aside to ANTONIO] The next advantage
Will we take throughly.

ANTONIO: [Aside to SEBASTIAN] Let it be to-night;
For, now they are oppress'd with travel, they
Will not, nor cannot, use such vigilance
As when they are fresh.

SEBASTIAN: [Aside to ANTONIO] I say, to-night: no more.

[*Solemn and strange music*]

ALONSO: What harmony is this? My good friends, hark!

GONZALO: Marvellous sweet music!

[*Enter PROSPERO above, invisible. Enter below*

several strange Shapes, bringing in a banquet;
they dance about it with gentle actions of
salutation; and, inviting the King, etc. to eat, they
depart]

ALONSO: Give us kind keepers, heavens! What
were these?

SEBASTIAN: A living drollery. Now I will believe
That there are unicorns, that in Arabia
There is one tree, the phoenix' throne, one
phoenix
At this hour reigning there.

ANTONIO: I'll believe both;
And what does else want credit, come to me,
And I'll be sworn 'tis true: travellers ne'er did lie,
Though fools at home condemn 'em.

GONZALO: If in Naples
I should report this now, would they believe me?
If I should say, I saw such islanders-
For, certes, these are people of the island-
Who, though they are of monstrous shape, yet,
note,
Their manners are more gentle-kind than of
Our human generation you shall find
Many, nay, almost any.

PROSPERO: [Aside] Honest lord,

Thou hast said well; for some of you there present

Are worse than devils.

ALONSO: I cannot too much muse

Such shapes, such gesture and such sound, expressing,

Although they want the use of tongue, a kind

Of excellent dumb discourse.

PROSPERO: [Aside] Praise in departing.

FRANCISCO: They vanish'd strangely.

SEBASTIAN: No matter, since

They have left their viands behind; for we have stomachs.

Will't please you taste of what is here?

ALONSO: Not I.

GONZALO: Faith, sir, you need not fear. When we were boys,

Who would believe that there were mountaineers

Dew-lapp'd like bulls, whose throats had hanging at 'em

Wallets of flesh? or that there were such men

Whose heads stood in their breasts? which now we find

Each putter-out of five for one will bring us

Good warrant of.

ALONSO: I will stand to and feed,

Although my last: no matter, since I feel

The best is past. Brother, my lord the duke,

Stand to and do as we.

[*Thunder and lightning. Enter ARIEL, like a
harpy; claps his wings upon the table; and, with a
quaint device, the banquet vanishes*]

ARIEL: You are three men of sin, whom Destiny,

That hath to instrument this lower world

And what is in't, the never-surfeited sea

Hath caused to belch up you; and on this island

Where man doth not inhabit; you 'mongst men

Being most unfit to live. I have made you mad;

And even with such-like valour men hang and
drown

Their proper selves.

[*ALONSO, SEBASTIAN etc. draw their swords*]

You fools! I and my fellows

Are ministers of Fate: the elements,

Of whom your swords are temper'd, may as well

Wound the loud winds, or with bemock'd-at stabs

Kill the still-closing waters, as diminish

One dowle that's in my plume: my fellow-
ministers
Are like invulnerable. If you could hurt,
Your swords are now too massy for your
strengths
And will not be uplifted. But remember-
For that's my business to you-that you three
From Milan did supplant good Prospero;
Exposed unto the sea, which hath requit it,
Him and his innocent child: for which foul deed
The powers, delaying, not forgetting, have
Incensed the seas and shores, yea, all the
creatures,
Against your peace. Thee of thy son, Alonso,
They have bereft; and do pronounce by me:
Lingering perdition, worse than any death
Can be at once, shall step by step attend
You and your ways; whose wraths to guard you
from-
Which here, in this most desolate isle, else falls
Upon your heads-is nothing but heart-sorrow
And a clear life ensuing.
[*He vanishes in thunder; then, to soft music,
enter the Shapes again, and dance, with mocks*

and mows, and carrying out the table]

PROSPERO: Bravely the figure of this harpy
hast thou

Perform'd, my Ariel; a grace it had, devouring:

Of my instruction hast thou nothing bated

In what thou hadst to say: so, with good life

And observation strange, my meaner ministers

Their several kinds have done. My high charms
work

And these mine enemies are all knit up

In their distractions; they now are in my power;

And in these fits I leave them, while I visit

Young Ferdinand, whom they suppose is
drown'd,

And his and mine loved darling.

[*Exit above*]

GONZALO: I' the name of something holy, sir,
why stand you

In this strange stare?

ALONSO: O, it is monstrous, monstrous:

Methought the billows spoke and told me of it;

The winds did sing it to me, and the thunder,

That deep and dreadful organ-pipe, pronounced

The name of Prosper: it did bass my trespass.

Therefore my son i' the ooze is bedded, and

I'll seek him deeper than e'er plummet sounded

And with him there lie mudded.

[*Exit*]

SEBASTIAN: But one fiend at a time,

I'll fight their legions o'er.

ANTONIO: I'll be thy second.

[*Exeunt SEBASTIAN, and ANTONIO*]

GONZALO: All three of them are desperate:

their great guilt,

Like poison given to work a great time after,

Now 'gins to bite the spirits. I do beseech you

That are of suppler joints, follow them swiftly

And hinder them from what this ecstasy

May now provoke them to.

ADRIAN: Follow, I pray you.

[*Exeunt*]

My Notes

ACT IV

SCENE I – Before Prospero's cell.

[*Enter PROSPERO, FERDINAND, and MIRANDA*]

PROSPERO: If I have too austerely punish'd you,

Your compensation makes amends, for I

Have given you here a third of mine own life,

Or that for which I live; who once again

I tender to thy hand: all thy vexations

Were but my trials of thy love and thou

Hast strangely stood the test here, afore Heaven,

I ratify this my rich gift. O Ferdinand,

Do not smile at me that I boast her off,

For thou shalt find she will outstrip all praise

And make it halt behind her.

FERDINAND: I do believe it

Against an oracle.

PROSPERO: Then, as my gift and thine own acquisition

Worthily purchased take my daughter: but

If thou dost break her virgin-knot before

All sanctimonious ceremonies may

With full and holy rite be minister'd,

No sweet aspersion shall the heavens let fall

To make this contract grow: but barren hate,

Sour-eyed disdain and discord shall bestrew

The union of your bed with weeds so loathly

That you shall hate it both: therefore take heed,

As Hymen's lamps shall light you.

FERDINAND: As I hope

For quiet days, fair issue and long life,

With such love as 'tis now, the murkiest den,

The most opportune place, the strong'st

suggestion.

Our worser genius can, shall never melt

Mine honour into lust, to take away

The edge of that day's celebration

When I shall think: or Phoebus' steeds are

founder'd,

Or Night kept chain'd below.

PROSPERO: Fairly spoke.

Sit then and talk with her; she is thine own.

What, Ariel! my industrious servant, Ariel!

[*Enter ARIEL*]

ARIEL: What would my potent master? here I

am.

PROSPERO: Thou and thy meaner fellows your last service

Did worthily perform; and I must use you

In such another trick. Go bring the rabble,

O'er whom I give thee power, here to this place:

Incite them to quick motion; for I must

Bestow upon the eyes of this young couple

Some vanity of mine art: it is my promise,

And they expect it from me.

ARIEL: Presently?

PROSPERO: Ay, with a twink.

ARIEL: Before you can say 'come' and 'go,'

And breathe twice and cry 'so, so,'

Each one, tripping on his toe,

Will be here with mop and mow.

Do you love me, master? no?

PROSPERO: Dearly my delicate Ariel. Do not approach

Till thou dost hear me call.

ARIEL: Well, I conceive.

[*Exit*]

PROSPERO: Look thou be true; do not give dalliance

Too much the rein: the strongest oaths are straw

To the fire i' the blood: be more abstemious,

Or else, good night your vow!

FERDINAND: I warrant you sir;

The white cold virgin snow upon my heart

Abates the ardour of my liver.

PROSPERO: Well.

Now come, my Ariel! bring a corollary,

Rather than want a spirit: appear and pertly!

No tongue! all eyes! be silent.

[*Soft music*]

[*Enter IRIS*]

IRIS: Ceres, most bounteous lady, thy rich leas

Of wheat, rye, barley, vetches, oats and peas;

Thy turfy mountains, where live nibbling sheep,

And flat meads thatch'd with stover, them to

keep;

Thy banks with pioned and twilled brims,

Which spongy April at thy hest betrims,

To make cold nymphs chaste crowns; and thy

broom-groves,

Whose shadow the dismissed bachelor loves,

Being lass-lorn: thy pole-clipt vineyard;

And thy sea-marge, sterile and rocky-hard,

Where thou thyself dost air;-the queen o' the sky,

Whose watery arch and messenger am I,

Bids thee leave these, and with her sovereign grace,

Here on this grass-plot, in this very place,

To come and sport: her peacocks fly amain:

Approach, rich Ceres, her to entertain.

[*Enter CERES*]

CERES: Hail, many-colour'd messenger, that ne'er

Dost disobey the wife of Jupiter;

Who with thy saffron wings upon my flowers

Diffusest honey-drops, refreshing showers,

And with each end of thy blue bow dost crown

My bosky acres and my unshrubb'd down,

Rich scarf to my proud earth; why hath thy queen

Summon'd me hither, to this short-grass'd green?

IRIS: A contract of true love to celebrate;

And some donation freely to estate

On the blest lovers.

CERES: Tell me, heavenly bow,

If Venus or her son, as thou dost know,

Do now attend the queen? Since they did plot

The means that dusky Dis my daughter got,

Her and her blind boy's scandal'd company

I have forsworn.

IRIS: Of her society

Be not afraid: I met her deity

Cutting the clouds towards Paphos and her son

Dove-drawn with her. Here thought they to have

done

Some wanton charm upon this man and maid,

Whose vows are, that no bed-right shall be paid

Till Hymen's torch be lighted: but vain;

Mars's hot minion is returned again;

Her waspish-headed son has broke his arrows,

Swears he will shoot no more but play with

sparrows

And be a boy right out.

CERES: High'st queen of state,

Great Juno, comes; I know her by her gait.

[*Enter JUNO*]

JUNO: How does my bounteous sister? Go with

me

To bless this twain, that they may prosperous be

And honour'd in their issue.

[*They sing:*]

JUNO: *Honour, riches, marriage-blessing,*

Long continuance, and increasing,

Hourly joys be still upon you!

Juno sings her blessings upon you.

CERES: *Earth's increase, foison plenty,*

Barns and garners never empty,

Vines and clustering bunches growing,

Plants with goodly burden bowing;

Spring come to you at the farthest

In the very end of harvest!

Scarcity and want shall shun you;

Ceres' blessing so is on you.

FERDINAND: This is a most majestic vision, and

Harmoniously charmingly. May I be bold

To think these spirits?

PROSPERO: Spirits, which by mine art

I have from their confines call'd to enact

My present fancies.

FERDINAND: Let me live here ever;

So rare a wonder'd father and a wife

Makes this place Paradise.

[*Juno and Ceres whisper, and send Iris on employment*]

PROSPERO: Sweet, now, silence!

Juno and Ceres whisper seriously;

There's something else to do: hush, and be

mute,

Or else our spell is marr'd.

IRIS: You nymphs, call'd Naiads, of the windring

brooks,

With your sedged crowns and ever-harmless

looks,

Leave your crisp channels and on this green land

Answer your summons; Juno does command:

Come, temperate nymphs, and help to celebrate

A contract of true love; be not too late.

[*Enter certain Nymphs*]

You sunburnt sicklemen, of August weary,

Come hither from the furrow and be merry:

Make holiday; your rye-straw hats put on

And these fresh nymphs encounter every one

In country footing.

[*Enter certain Reapers, properly habited: they*

join with the Nymphs in a graceful dance;

towards the end whereof PROSPERO starts

suddenly, and speaks; after which, to a strange,

hollow, and confused noise, they heavily vanish]

PROSPERO: [Aside] I had forgot that foul

conspiracy

Of the beast Caliban and his confederates

Against my life: the minute of their plot

Is almost come.

[*To the Spirits*]

Well done! avoid; no more!

FERDINAND: This is strange: your father's in

some passion

That works him strongly.

MIRANDA: Never till this day

Saw I him touch'd with anger so distemper'd.

PROSPERO: You do look, my son, in a moved

sort,

As if you were dismay'd: be cheerful, sir.

Our revels now are ended. These our actors,

As I foretold you, were all spirits and

Are melted into air, into thin air:

And, like the baseless fabric of this vision,

The cloud-capp'd towers, the gorgeous palaces,

The solemn temples, the great globe itself,

Ye all which it inherit, shall dissolve

And, like this insubstantial pageant faded,

Leave not a rack behind. We are such stuff

As dreams are made on, and our little life

Is rounded with a sleep. Sir, I am vex'd;

Bear with my weakness; my, brain is troubled:

Be not disturb'd with my infirmity:

If you be pleased, retire into my cell

And there repose: a turn or two I'll walk,

To still my beating mind.

FERDINAND and MIRANDA: We wish your
peace.

[*Exeunt*]

PROSPERO: Come with a thought I thank thee,
Ariel: come.

[*Enter ARIEL*]

ARIEL: Thy thoughts I cleave to. What's thy
pleasure?

PROSPERO: Spirit,

We must prepare to meet with Caliban.

ARIEL: Ay, my commander: when I presented
Ceres,

I thought to have told thee of it, but I fear'd

Lest I might anger thee.

PROSPERO: Say again, where didst thou leave
these varlets?

ARIEL: I told you, sir, they were red-hot with
drinking;

So fun of valour that they smote the air

For breathing in their faces; beat the ground

For kissing of their feet; yet always bending

Towards their project. Then I beat my tabor;

At which, like unback'd colts, they prick'd
their ears,

Advanced their eyelids, lifted up their noses

As they smelt music: so I charm'd their ears

That calf-like they my lowing follow'd through

Tooth'd briers, sharp furzes, pricking goss and
thorns,

Which entered their frail shins: at last I left them

I' the filthy-mantled pool beyond your cell,

There dancing up to the chins, that the foul lake

O'erstunk their feet.

PROSPERO: This was well done, my bird.

Thy shape invisible retain thou still:

The trumpery in my house, go bring it hither,

For stale to catch these thieves.

ARIEL: I go, I go.

[*Exit*]

PROSPERO: A devil, a born devil, on whose
nature

Nurture can never stick; on whom my pains,

Humanely taken, all, all lost, quite lost;

And as with age his body uglier grows,

So his mind cankers. I will plague them all,

Even to roaring.

[*Re-enter ARIEL, loaden with glistering apparel,*
etc]

Come, hang them on this line.

[*PROSPERO and ARIEL remain invisible. Enter*
CALIBAN, STEPHANO, and TRINCULO, all wet]

CALIBAN: Pray you, tread softly, that the blind
mole may not

Hear a foot fall: we now are near his cell.

STEPHANO: Monster, your fairy, which you say
is a harmless fairy, has done little better than
played the Jack with us.

TRINCULO: Monster, I do smell all horse-piss; at
which my nose is in great indignation.

STEPHANO: So is mine. Do you hear, monster?
If I should take a displeasure against you, look
you,-

TRINCULO: Thou wert but a lost monster.

CALIBAN: Good my lord, give me thy favour
still.

Be patient, for the prize I'll bring thee to

Shall hoodwink this mischance: therefore speak softly.

All's hush'd as midnight yet.

TRINCULO: Ay, but to lose our bottles in the pool,-

STEPHANO: There is not only disgrace and dishonour in that, monster, but an infinite loss.

TRINCULO: That's more to me than my wetting: yet this is your harmless fairy, monster.

STEPHANO: I will fetch off my bottle, though I be o'er ears for my labour.

CALIBAN: Prithee, my king, be quiet. Seest thou here,

This is the mouth o' the cell: no noise, and enter.

Do that good mischief which may make this island

Thine own for ever, and I, thy Caliban,

For aye thy foot-licker.

STEPHANO: Give me thy hand. I do begin to have bloody thoughts.

TRINCULO: O king Stephano! O peer! O worthy Stephano! Look what a wardrobe here is for thee!

CALIBAN: Let it alone, thou fool; it is but trash.

TRINCULO: O, ho, monster! we know what belongs to a frippery. O king Stephano!

STEPHANO: Put off that gown, Trinculo; by this hand, I'll have that gown.

TRINCULO: Thy grace shall have it.

CALIBAN: The dropsy drown this fool I what do you mean
To dote thus on such luggage? Let's alone
And do the murder first: if he awake,
From toe to crown he'll fill our skins with pinches,
Make us strange stuff.

STEPHANO: Be you quiet, monster. Mistress line, is not this my jerkin? Now is the jerkin under the line: now, jerkin, you are like to lose your hair and prove a bald jerkin.

TRINCULO: Do, do: we steal by line and level, an't like your grace.

STEPHANO: I thank thee for that jest; here's a garment for't: wit shall not go unrewarded while I am king of this country. 'Steal by line and level' is an excellent pass of pate; there's another garment for't.

TRINCULO: Monster, come, put some lime upon your fingers, and away with the rest.

CALIBAN: I will have none on't: we shall lose our time,

And all be turn'd to barnacles, or to apes

With foreheads villanous low.

STEPHANO: Monster, lay-to your fingers: help to bear this away where my hogshead of wine is, or I'll turn you out of my kingdom: go to, carry this.

TRINCULO: And this.

STEPHANO: Ay, and this.

[*A noise of hunters heard. Enter divers Spirits, in shape of hounds, and hunt them about, PROSPERO and ARIEL setting them on*]

PROSPERO: Hey, Mountain, hey!

ARIEL: Silver! there it goes, Silver!

PROSPERO: Fury, Fury! there, Tyrant, there! hark! hark!

[*CALIBAN, STEPHANO, and TRINCULO, are driven out*]

Go charge my goblins that they grind their joints

With dry convulsions, shorten up their sinews

With aged cramps, and more pinch-spotted make them

Than pard or cat o' mountain.

ARIEL: Hark, they roar!

PROSPERO: Let them be hunted soundly. At
this hour
Lie at my mercy all mine enemies:
Shortly shall all my labours end, and thou
Shalt have the air at freedom: for a little
Follow, and do me service.

[*Exeunt*]

My Notes

ACT V

[*Enter PROSPERO in his magic robes, and ARIEL*]

PROSPERO: Now does my project gather to a head:

My charms crack not; my spirits obey; and time

Goes upright with his carriage. How's the day?

ARIEL: On the sixth hour; at which time, my lord,

You said our work should cease.

PROSPERO: I did say so,

When first I raised the tempest. Say, my spirit,

How fares the king and 's followers?

ARIEL: Confined together

In the same fashion as you gave in charge,

Just as you left them; all prisoners, sir,

In the line-grove which weather-fends your cell;

They cannot budge till your release. The king,

His brother and yours, abide all three distracted

And the remainder mourning over them,

Brimful of sorrow and dismay; but chiefly

Him that you term'd, sir, 'The good old lord

Gonzalo;'

His tears run down his beard, like winter's drops

From eaves of reeds. Your charm so strongly works 'em

That if you now beheld them, your affections

Would become tender.

PROSPERO: Dost thou think so, spirit?

ARIEL: Mine would, sir, were I human.

PROSPERO: And mine shall.

Hast thou, which art but air, a touch, a feeling

Of their afflictions, and shall not myself,

One of their kind, that relish all as sharply,

Passion as they, be kindlier moved than thou art?

Though with their high wrongs I am struck to the quick,

Yet with my nobler reason 'gaitist my fury

Do I take part: the rarer action is

In virtue than in vengeance: they being penitent,

The sole drift of my purpose doth extend

Not a frown further. Go release them, Ariel:

My charms I'll break, their senses I'll restore,

And they shall be themselves.

ARIEL: I'll fetch them, sir.

[Exit]

PROSPERO: Ye elves of hills, brooks, standing lakes and groves,

And ye that on the sands with printless foot

Do chase the ebbing Neptune and do fly him

When he comes back; you demi-puppets that

By moonshine do the green sour ringlets make,

Whereof the ewe not bites, and you whose pastime

Is to make midnight mushrooms, that rejoice

To hear the solemn curfew; by whose aid,

Weak masters though ye be, I have bedimm'd

The noontide sun, call'd forth the mutinous winds,

And 'twixt the green sea and the azured vault

Set roaring war: to the dread rattling thunder

Have I given fire and rifted Jove's stout oak

With his own bolt; the strong-based promontory

Have I made shake and by the spurs pluck'd up

The pine and cedar: graves at my command

Have waked their sleepers, oped, and let 'em forth

By my so potent art. But this rough magic

I here abjure, and, when I have required

Some heavenly music, which even now I do,
To work mine end upon their senses that
This airy charm is for, I'll break my staff,
Bury it certain fathoms in the earth,
And deeper than did ever plummet sound
I'll drown my book.

[*Solemn music*]

[*Re-enter ARIEL: then ALONSO, with a frantic gesture, attended by GONZALO; SEBASTIAN and ANTONIO in like manner, attended by ADRIAN and FRANCISCO: they all enter the circle which PROSPERO had made, and there stand charmed; which PROSPERO observing, speaks:*]

A solemn air and the best comforter
To an unsettled fancy cure thy brains,
Now useless, boil'd within thy skull! There stand,
For you are spell-stopp'd.
Holy Gonzalo, honourable man,
Mine eyes, even sociable to the show of thine,
Fall fellowly drops. The charm dissolves apace,
And as the morning steals upon the night,
Melting the darkness, so their rising senses
Begin to chase the ignorant fumes that mantle

Their clearer reason. O good Gonzalo,
My true preserver, and a loyal sir
To him you follow'st! I will pay thy graces
Home both in word and deed. Most cruelly
Didst thou, Alonso, use me and my daughter:
Thy brother was a furtherer in the act.
Thou art pinch'd fort now, Sebastian. Flesh and
blood,
You, brother mine, that entertain'd ambition,
Expell'd remorse and nature; who, with
Sebastian,
Whose inward pinches therefore are most
strong,
Would here have kill'd your king; I do forgive
thee,
Unnatural though thou art. Their understanding
Begins to swell, and the approaching tide
Will shortly fill the reasonable shore
That now lies foul and muddy. Not one of them
That yet looks on me, or would know me Ariel,
Fetch me the hat and rapier in my cell:
I will discase me, and myself present
As I was sometime Milan: quickly, spirit;
Thou shalt ere long be free.

[ARIEL sings and helps to attire PROSPERO]

Where the bee sucks. there suck I:

In a cowslip's bell I lie;

There I couch when owls do cry.

On the bat's back I do fly

After summer merrily.

Merrily, merrily shall I live now

Under the blossom that hangs on the bough.

PROSPERO: Why, that's my dainty Ariel! I shall miss thee:

But yet thou shalt have freedom: so, so, so.

To the king's ship, invisible as thou art:

There shalt thou find the mariners asleep

Under the hatches; the master and the boatswain

Being awake, enforce them to this place,

And presently, I prithee.

ARIEL: I drink the air before me, and return

Or ere your pulse twice beat.

[Exit]

GONZALO: All torment, trouble, wonder and amazement

Inhabits here: some heavenly power guide us

Out of this fearful country!

PROSPERO: Behold, sir king,

The wronged Duke of Milan, Prospero:

For more assurance that a living prince

Does now speak to thee, I embrace thy body;

And to thee and thy company I bid

A hearty welcome.

ALONSO: Whether thou best he or no,

Or some enchanted trifle to abuse me,

As late I have been, I not know: thy pulse

Beats as of flesh and blood; and, since I saw

thee,

The affliction of my mind amends, with which,

I fear, a madness held me: this must crave,

An if this be at all, a most strange story.

Thy dukedom I resign and do entreat

Thou pardon me my wrongs. But how should

Prospero

Be living and be here?

PROSPERO: First, noble friend,

Let me embrace thine age, whose honour cannot

Be measured or confined.

GONZALO: Whether this be

Or be not, I'll not swear.

PROSPERO: You do yet taste

Some subtilties o' the isle, that will not let you
Believe things certain. Welcome, my friends all!
[*Aside to SEBASTIAN and ANTONIO*]
But you, my brace of lords, were I so minded,
I here could pluck his highness' frown upon you
And justify you traitors: at this time
I will tell no tales.

SEBASTIAN: [Aside] The devil speaks in him.

PROSPERO: No.
For you, most wicked sir, whom to call brother
Would even infect my mouth, I do forgive
Thy rankest fault; all of them; and require
My dukedom of thee, which perforce, I know,
Thou must restore.

ALONSO: If thou be'st Prospero,
Give us particulars of thy preservation;
How thou hast met us here, who three hours since
Were wreck'd upon this shore; where I have lost-
How sharp the point of this remembrance is!-
My dear son Ferdinand.

PROSPERO: I am woe for't, sir.

ALONSO: Irreparable is the loss, and patience
Says it is past her cure.

PROSPERO: I rather think

You have not sought her help, of whose soft grace

For the like loss I have her sovereign aid

And rest myself content.

ALONSO: You the like loss!

PROSPERO: As great to me as late; and, supportable

To make the dear loss, have I means much weaker

Than you may call to comfort you, for I

Have lost my daughter.

ALONSO: A daughter?

O heavens, that they were living both in Naples,

The king and queen there! that they were, I wish

Myself were mudded in that oozy bed

Where my son lies. When did you lose your daughter?

PROSPERO: In this last tempest. I perceive these lords

At this encounter do so much admire

That they devour their reason and scarce think

Their eyes do offices of truth, their words

Are natural breath: but, howsoe'er you have

Been justled from your senses, know for certain

That I am Prospero and that very duke

Which was thrust forth of Milan, who most
strangely

Upon this shore, where you were wreck'd, was
landed,

To be the lord on't. No more yet of this;

For 'tis a chronicle of day by day,

Not a relation for a breakfast nor

Befitting this first meeting. Welcome, sir;

This cell's my court: here have I few attendants

And subjects none abroad: pray you, look in.

My dukedom since you have given me again,

I will requite you with as good a thing;

At least bring forth a wonder, to content ye

As much as me my dukedom.

[*Here PROSPERO discovers FERDINAND and
MIRANDA playing at chess*]

MIRANDA: Sweet lord, you play me false.

FERDINAND: No, my dear'st love,

I would not for the world.

MIRANDA: Yes, for a score of kingdoms you
should wrangle,

And I would call it, fair play.

ALONSO: If this prove

A vision of the Island, one dear son

Shall I twice lose.

SEBASTIAN: A most high miracle!

FERDINAND: Though the seas threaten, they

are merciful;

I have cursed them without cause.

[*Kneels*]

ALONSO: Now all the blessings

Of a glad father compass thee about!

Arise, and say how thou camest here.

MIRANDA: O, wonder!

How many goodly creatures are there here!

How beauteous mankind is! O brave new world,

That has such people in't!

PROSPERO: 'Tis new to thee.

ALONSO: What is this maid with whom thou

wast at play?

Your eld'st acquaintance cannot be three hours:

Is she the goddess that hath sever'd us,

And brought us thus together?

FERDINAND: Sir, she is mortal;

But by immortal Providence she's mine:

I chose her when I could not ask my father

For his advice, nor thought I had one. She

Is daughter to this famous Duke of Milan,

Of whom so often I have heard renown,

But never saw before; of whom I have

Received a second life; and second father

This lady makes him to me.

ALONSO: I am hers:

But, O, how oddly will it sound that I

Must ask my child forgiveness!

PROSPERO: There, sir, stop:

Let us not burden our remembrance with

A heaviness that's gone.

GONZALO: I have inly wept,

Or should have spoke ere this. Look down, you god,

And on this couple drop a blessed crown!

For it is you that have chalk'd forth the way

Which brought us hither.

ALONSO: I say, Amen, Gonzalo!

GONZALO: Was Milan thrust from Milan, that his issue

Should become kings of Naples? O, rejoice

Beyond a common joy, and set it down

With gold on lasting pillars: In one voyage

Did Claribel her husband find at Tunis,

And Ferdinand, her brother, found a wife

Where he himself was lost, Prospero his

dukedom

In a poor isle and all of us ourselves

When no man was his own.

ALONSO: [To FERDINAND and MIRANDA]

Give me your hands:

Let grief and sorrow still embrace his heart

That doth not wish you joy!

GONZALO: Be it so! Amen!

[*Re-enter ARIEL, with the Master and Boatswain*

amazedly following]

O, look, sir, look, sir! here is more of us:

I prophesied, if a gallows were on land,

This fellow could not drown. Now, blasphemy,

That swear'st grace o'erboard, not an oath on

shore?

Hast thou no mouth by land? What is the news?

Boatswain: The best news is, that we have

safely found

Our king and company; the next, our ship-

Which, but three glasses since, we gave out

split-

Is tight and yare and bravely rigg'd as when
We first put out to sea.

ARIEL: [Aside to PROSPERO] Sir, all this service

Have I done since I went.

PROSPERO: [Aside to ARIEL] My tricksy spirit!

ALONSO: These are not natural events; they strengthen

From strange to stranger. Say, how came you hither?

Boatswain: If I did think, sir, I were well awake,
I'ld strive to tell you. We were dead of sleep,
And-how we know not-all clapp'd under hatches;
Where but even now with strange and several noises
Of roaring, shrieking, howling, jingling chains,
And more diversity of sounds, all horrible,
We were awaked; straightway, at liberty;
Where we, in all her trim, freshly beheld
Our royal, good and gallant ship, our master
Capering to eye her: on a trice, so please you,
Even in a dream, were we divided from them
And were brought moping hither.

ARIEL: [Aside to PROSPERO] Was't well done?

PROSPERO: [Aside to ARIEL] Bravely, my

diligence. Thou shalt be free.

ALONSO: This is as strange a maze as e'er men

trod

And there is in this business more than nature

Was ever conduct of: some oracle

Must rectify our knowledge.

PROSPERO: Sir, my liege,

Do not infest your mind with beating on

The strangeness of this business; at pick'd

leisure

Which shall be shortly, single I'll resolve you,

Which to you shall seem probable, of every

These happen'd accidents; till when, be cheerful

And think of each thing well.

[*Aside to ARIEL*]

Come hither, spirit:

Set Caliban and his companions free;

Untie the spell.

[*Exit ARIEL*]

How fares my gracious sir?

There are yet missing of your company

Some few odd lads that you remember not.

[*Re-enter ARIEL, driving in CALIBAN,*

STEPHANO and TRINCULO, in their stolen apparel]

STEPHANO: Every man shift for all the rest, and let no man take care for himself; for all is but fortune. Coragio, bully-monster, coragio!

TRINCULO: If these be true spies which I wear in my head, here's a goodly sight.

CALIBAN: O Setebos, these be brave spirits indeed!

How fine my master is! I am afraid

He will chastise me.

SEBASTIAN: Ha, ha!

What things are these, my lord Antonio?

Will money buy 'em?

ANTONIO: Very like; one of them

Is a plain fish, and, no doubt, marketable.

PROSPERO: Mark but the badges of these men, my lords,

Then say if they be true. This mis-shapen knave,

His mother was a witch, and one so strong

That could control the moon, make flows and ebbs,

And deal in her command without her power.

These three have robb'd me; and this demi-devil-

For he's a bastard one-had plotted with them
To take my life. Two of these fellows you
Must know and own; this thing of darkness!
Acknowledge mine.

CALIBAN: I shall be pinch'd to death.

ALONSO: Is not this Stephano, my drunken
butler?

SEBASTIAN: He is drunk now: where had he
wine?

ALONSO: And Trinculo is reeling ripe: where
should they
Find this grand liquor that hath gilded 'em?
How camest thou in this pickle?

TRINCULO: I have been in such a pickle since I
saw you last that, I fear me, will never out of my
bones: I shall not fear fly-blowing.

SEBASTIAN: Why, how now, Stephano!

STEPHANO: O, touch me not; I am not
Stephano, but a cramp.

PROSPERO: You'ld be king o' the isle, sirrah?

STEPHANO: I should have been a sore one
then.

ALONSO: This is a strange thing as e'er I look'd
on.

[Pointing to Caliban]

PROSPERO: He is as disproportion'd in his manners

As in his shape. Go, sirrah, to my cell;

Take with you your companions; as you look

To have my pardon, trim it handsomely.

CALIBAN: Ay, that I will; and I'll be wise hereafter

And seek for grace. What a thrice-double ass

Was I, to take this drunkard for a god

And worship this dull fool!

PROSPERO: Go to; away!

ALONSO: Hence, and bestow your luggage where you found it.

SEBASTIAN: Or stole it, rather.

[Exeunt CALIBAN, STEPHANO, and TRINCULO]

PROSPERO: Sir, I invite your highness and your train

To my poor cell, where you shall take your rest

For this one night; which, part of it, I'll waste

With such discourse as, I not doubt, shall make it

Go quick away; the story of my life

And the particular accidents gone by

Since I came to this isle: and in the morn

I'll bring you to your ship and so to Naples,

Where I have hope to see the nuptial

Of these our dear-beloved solemnized;

And thence retire me to my Milan, where

Every third thought shall be my grave.

ALONSO: I long

To hear the story of your life, which must

Take the ear strangely.

PROSPERO: I'll deliver all;

And promise you calm seas, auspicious gales

And sail so expeditious that shall catch

Your royal fleet far off.

[*Aside to ARIEL*]

My Ariel, chick,

That is thy charge: then to the elements

Be free, and fare thou well! Please you, draw

near.

[*Exeunt*]

EPILOGUE

Spoken by Prospero

Now my charms are all o'erthrown,
And what strength I have's mine own,
Which is most faint: now, 'tis true,
I must be here confined by you,
Or sent to Naples. Let me not,
Since I have my dukedom got
And pardon'd the deceiver, dwell
In this bare island by your spell;
But release me from my bands
With the help of your good hands:
Gentle breath of yours my sails
Must fill, or else my project fails,
Which was to please. Now I want
Spirits to enforce, art to enchant,
And my ending is despair,
Unless I be relieved by prayer,
Which pierces so that it assaults
Mercy itself and frees all faults.
As you from crimes would pardon'd be,
Let your indulgence set me free.

My Notes

Glossary of Literary Terms

Alliteration: The occurrence of identical sounds, most often at the beginning of words e.g. "From forth the fatal loins of these two foes"

Allusion: An indirect reference to something

Anaphora: Repetition of the same word or phrase at the beginning of consecutive lines

Antagonist: The **protagonist**'s main adversary.

Antithesis: A person or thing that is the opposite of something else

Aside: A character's remark that is only meant to be heard by the audience but unheard by other characters in the play

Assonance: The resemblance of sounds between vowels of words in close proximity to one another

Blank verse: **Poetry** written with a regular **metre** but unrhymed, almost always in **iambic pentameter**

Climax: The dramatic end to the main **plot**. This is usually followed by **falling action**

Couplet: Two successive rhyming lines

Dramatic monologue: A poem in the form of a speech of an individual character

Euphemism: A gentle way of expressing something unpleasant

Falling Action: The section of a story following the **climax** but before the very end of the story

Foil: A character providing a contrast with another

Foot: A combination of stressed and unstressed syllables

Heroic couplet: a pair of rhyming **iambic pentameters**

Hyperbole: Exaggerated statements not meant to be taken literally

Iambic pentameter: A line of verse with five metrical feet, each consisting of one unstressed syllable followed by one stressed syllable

Imagery: A visually descriptive use of language

Internal rhyme: A rhyme involving a word in the middle of a line

Metaphor: A figure of speech that applies words to describe something in a non-literal way (e.g. *coal black eyes*). Metaphors do not use the words "like" or "as". If these words are used it is a **simile** (e.g. *eyes as black as coal*, or *eyes like black coal*).

Metre: The basic rhythmic structure of a verse or lines in a verse

Motif: An image or idea that runs through a play or novel

Onomatopoeia: A word that resembles the sound it is describing e.g. cuckoo, woof, burp, etc

Oxymoron: A figure of speech containing contradictory words, e.g. deafening silence

Paradox: A statement that contradicts itself e.g "This sentence is not true"

Personification: Attributing human characteristics to inanimate things

Plot: The events that make up the main part of a story

Poetry: Rhymed or rhythmic text

Pronoun: Referring to a person or thing, e.g. I, you, she, this, that

Prose: Written or spoken language without rhyme or rhythm

Protagonist: The lead character

Quatrain: A **stanza** of four lines

Refrain: A word or series of words repeated at intervals within a poem

Simile: A figure of speech containing "as" or "like" to describe something in a non-literal way (e.g. eyes like black coal). If the words "like" or "as" are not used then it is a **metaphor** (e.g. coal black eyes).

Soliloquy: A speech spoken by a character when alone, revealing their innermost thoughts

Sonnet: A fourteen-line poem.

Stanza: A group of poetic lines resembling paragraphs in **prose**

Sub-plot: A plot separate to the main **plot**

Syntax: The arrangement of words and phrases within a sentence

Tragic Hero: Generally the **protagonist** whose flaws or mistakes lead to their downfall

The Tempest Glossary

Abstemious – Moderate or temperate

Amain – At full speed

Bark – A small sailing ship

Bermoothes – Archaic term for a collection of islands including Bermuda

Betid – Befell

Boatswain – A ship's officer, in charge of the deck crew

Bourn – Boundary or limit

Butt – Tub

By'r lakin – "By your ladykin"; a reference to the Virgin Mary

Chaps – Jaws

Chirugeonly – Surgeon

Coragio – Take courage

Dowle – Small feather

Dropsy – Bodily swelling due to excessive fluid

Extirpate – Destroy

Feater – Neater

Foil – Thwart

Foison – Plentiful harvest

Flote – Sea

Furze – Gorse

Gaberdine – Loose garment

Glut – Swallow

Hest – Command

Hollowly – Insincerely

Holp – Helped

Inch-meal – Inch by inch

Inveterate – Firmly established over a long period

Jerkin – A close-fitting jacket

Kibe – A sore, especially on the heel

Moon-calf – Monster

Murrain – Plague

Patch – Clown or fool

Phoebus – Greek god

Pied ninny – Fool

Rapier – Slender two-edged sword

Rate – Opinion

Requite – Respond to

Roarers – Noisy and unruly waves

Signories – The governing body that ruled over medieval city-states

Surety – A person who takes responsibility for another

Swabber – Sailor who cleans the ship's decks

Tawny – Brownish-yellow

Teen – Injury or harm

Too massy – Too heavy

Trident – Three-pronged spear

Trumpery – Showy but worthless

Twain – Two

Unbacked – Horse that has never been ridden

Unstanched – Immoral

Vanity – Illusion or trick

Varlet – Ruffian

Wallets – Hanging flesh, such as on turkeys' necks

Wezand – Windpipe

Whist – Silent

Yarely – Briskly

For more on our large print, dyslexia-friendly, and annotation-friendly books, as well as our bulk discounts for schools visit:

firestonebooks.com

Printed in Great Britain
by Amazon

45470907R00081